# Modern Varieties of Judaism

LECTURES ON THE HISTORY OF RELIGIONS
SPONSORED BY THE
AMERICAN COUNCIL OF LEARNED SOCIETIES
NEW SERIES, NUMBER EIGHT

# Modern Varieties of Judaism

JOSEPH L. BLAU

*Columbia University Press*

NEW YORK AND LONDON

Joseph L. Blau, Professor of Religion at Columbia University, is the author of *The Christian Interpretation of the Cabala in the Renaissance* (1945), *Social Theories of Jacksonian Democracy* (1947), *Cornerstones of Religious Freedom in America* (1949; rev. ed., 1964), *Men and Movements in American Philosophy* (1952), and *The Story of Jewish Philosophy* (1962), and the author, with Salo W. Baron, of *Judaism: Post-Biblical and Talmudic Periods* (1954). He is also the editor of *American Philosophic Addresses* (1946), joint editor of *Essays on Jewish Life and Thought* (1959), and joint editor, with Salo W. Baron, of *The Jews of the United States, 1790–1840: A Documentary History* (3 vols., 1964).

ISBN 0-231-02867-9 *clothbound*
ISBN 0-231-08668-7 *paperbound*

COPYRIGHT © 1964, 1966 COLUMBIA UNIVERSITY PRESS
PRINTED IN THE UNITED STATES OF AMERICA
LIBRARY OF CONGRESS CATALOG CARD NUMBER: 66-10732
9 8 7 6 5 4 3

*For* SALO WITTMAYER BARON

*preeminent among Jewish historians*

This volume is the eighth to be published in the series of Lectures on the History of Religions for which the American Council of Learned Societies, through its Committee on the History of Religions, assumed responsibility in 1936.

Under the program the Committee from time to time enlists the services of scholars to lecture in colleges, universities, and seminaries on topics in need of expert elucidation. Subsequently, when possible and appropriate, the Committee arranges for the publication of the lectures. Other volumes in the series are Martin P. Nilsson, *Greek Popular Religion* (1940), Henri Frankfort, *Ancient Egyptian Religion* (1948), Wing-tsit Chan, *Religious Trends in Modern China* (1953), Joachim Wach, *The Comparative Study of Religions,* edited by Joseph M. Kitagawa (1958), R. M. Grant, *Gnosticism and Early Christianity* (1959), Robert Lawson Slater, *World Religions and World Community* (1963), and Joseph M. Kitagawa, *Religion in Japanese History* (1966).

# Preface

This book is an expansion of six lectures prepared and delivered under the auspices of the Committee on the History of Religions of the American Council of Learned Societies. They were presented, either as a whole or in part, during the academic year 1964–65, at Northwestern University, Princeton University, Harvard Divinity School and Center for the Study of World Religions, Columbia University, the University of Chicago, Union Theological Seminary, Rice University, the Perkins Theological Seminary of Southern Methodist University, San Diego State College, Claremont Graduate School, the Southern California School of Theology, and Duke University. In several cases, the local B'nai B'rith-Hillel Foundation joined with the university in sponsoring the lectures. To the officers, members of the several faculties, Hillel directors, and students who helped to make the author's many trips pleasant as well as exhilarating, sincere thanks are due.

Closer to home, the author acknowledges with gratitude the generosity of Columbia University and of his colleagues in the Department of Religion for having freed so much of his time for the presentation of these lectures. Richard Levy and the author's wife, Eleanor W. Blau, have helped in supplying the documentation for this volume, and Miriam Buck gave the manuscript "tender loving care." Considerable sections of the materials used here were taken, with but slight emendations, from an article entitled "The Spiritual Life of American Jewry, 1654–1954," originally commissioned by the *American Jewish Yearbook,* and published in the *Yearbook* in 1955.

The basic hypothesis underlying my approach to the modern varieties of Judaism is that every living religion is perennially changing, adapting its principles, its practices, its rituals, its beliefs, and its theology to meet the needs of the varying times and places in which its adherents live. Each living religion *must* change thus, if it is to continue to have relevance to the lives of those who accept it. But, although it is constantly changing, each religion must seem to be as unchanging as possible, for though we want our religions to be always relevant, we also want them to serve as our link to the past, the root of our sense of continuity. Most of the time, therefore, changes in religions take place slowly, almost imperceptibly. From time to time, however, in the history of every religion, the conditions under which its adherents live change so rapidly and so radically that the changes in the religion must come with shocking rapidity.

Because the adherents of Judaism have moved with great frequency from one cultural environment to another, the shock and crisis of rapid change have occurred more frequently in the history of Judaism than in that of other living religions. Judaism has faced many crises, from each of which it has emerged with an altered countenance. The most recent of these crises, one from which Judaism is only now beginning to recover, was induced by its encounter with the modern world, chiefly in Western Europe and the United States of America. This latest crisis of adjustment to modernity is the subject of these lectures. My thesis is that all the movements in the Judaism of the last two centuries are, in one degree or another, responses to the modern world, attempts

to bring about radical change without destroying the sense
of continuity with an age-old past. I cannot begin to estimate
to what extent I owe this thesis and my ability to sustain it
to my association with my beloved teacher, Salo W. Baron,
an association of thirty-five years' standing. In dedicating
this book to him, I hope to signalize my debt to him; I can
never hope to repay it.

JOSEPH L. BLAU

*Columbia University*
*March, 1965*

# Contents

# Contents

*Modern Varieties of Judaism*

# Emancipation and
# the Birth of Modern Judaism

## THE MEDIEVAL JEWISH COMMUNITY

The gap between the Western European Jew and his non-Jewish neighbors was never as wide and impassable in practice as it was in theory.[1] From the very beginning of Jewish life in the Christian countries, it may be said that Jews played a double role in the general community. One of their parts was as figures in the Christian epic, in whose terms the Jews were the rejectors of Jesus Christ, the Saviour. They had reviled him and spat at him; they bore the responsibility for his crucifixion; they had consistently refused, even after the most evident proofs of his divinity, to yield in their stiff-necked and stubborn opposition to him. Down through the centuries, a vast majority of the Jews had preferred martyr-dom to conversion, when the choice was offered to them, and had gone to their deaths affirming the faith of their fathers in the absolute unity of God. For this opposition, so ran the theological account, it was necessary that the Jews should suffer punishment; yet it was equally important that, wher-ever possible, their lives should not be forfeited. Alive, the

Jews, in their misery, served as a visible witness to the sorry
fate of those who had had the chance to gain salvation
through the acceptance of the revelation of God in Jesus
Christ and had failed to take advantage of their great opportunity. The safest place in Europe for Jews to live, during
the middle ages, was in Rome, where they were under the
direct protection of the Supreme Pontiff.[2] Thus the Jews of
Europe were, theologically, not merely the eternal strangers
but the eternally estranged. As anti-Christians, they were the
allies of the Antichrist, child of Satan. As minions of Satan,
they were feared for their magical powers.[3]

In addition to this theological role, the Jews of Europe
played a positive part in the economic life of their times.
They were unable to diversify their economic activities across
the full spectrum, for restrictive laws precluded their participation in a number of important aspects of the European
economy.[4] Thus, for example, the low theological estate of
the Jews was taken as the basis for laws that asserted that it
was improper for Christians to work for them in subordinate
positions. Laws of this sort virtually excluded the Jews from
landowning and, as a consequence, from agriculture. From
this situation arose the myth, still prevalent in our own day,
that Jews are by nature unfit for agricultural pursuits. The
most characteristic effect of laws restricting the participation
of Jews in the economy of the middle ages was their entry
into those activities to which, for one reason or another,
Christians were not drawn; the Jews were, in a modern
phrase, marginal in the economy of the middle ages. The
economic theology of medieval Christianity made but scant
provision for typical middle-class activities; a narrow definition of usury made even normal commercial pursuits of du-
bious virtue and such necessary activities of society as bank-
ing and moneylending almost impossible for the faithful
Christian. The Jews provided, for much of Europe, an urban
middle class of traders, bankers, and moneylenders. They
eked out their own subsistence in the interstices of the eco-

nomic life of Europe, resented, as the middle class always is, by the peasant lower class, and subject to the constant threat of extortion and expropriation by the upper class.

Resented or not, Jewish commerce was essential and was one of the chief ways in which the Jew and his non-Jewish neighbor were in constant contact with each other. Other types of relationship were less frequent. Thus, for example, the progress of medical science was extremely retarded among medieval Christians; this is especially true of the progress of surgery. Jewish physicians, on the other hand, while they can by no means be compared with modern medical scientists, did keep abreast of the latest developments (chiefly those of Muslim physicians) and make important contributions to medicine of their times. So many medieval Christians preferred the services of Jewish physicians to those of Christians that a conciliar edict pronounced it illegal for Christians to be attended by Jewish physicians; the very pope, however, during whose reign this rule was enacted called in a Jewish physician when he was ill.[5] Once more we see that practical necessity contrived to bridge the theoretical chasm between Jew and non-Jew.

Both theologically, then, and economically, the Jews had a part to play in European society in medieval times. Theirs was not a life completely apart from that of their neighbors. Nevertheless the European Jew was a source of embarrassment within society, because he had no proper place in it. For the structure of society during the European middle ages was fixed. It followed the pattern of what Sir Henry Maine called "status society." Most briefly interpreted, Maine meant by this term a society in which the family is "the unit of which civil laws take account"; that is to say, a society in which a man's place is completely determined by the place held by his family.[6] Whether one approaches medieval society through political, economic, or religious studies, he is met by clear evidence of a hierarchy of status. Within this determinate pattern of social order, the Jews of Europe re-

sisted any comfortable or easy placement. The social order
within which they resided and in which they served important functions was a Christian order; as non-Christians they
could never be properly integrated into it. The Jews simply
did not belong.

Faced with the dilemma of having to provide a place in
status society for this status-less group, medieval society came
to some sort of resolution of the problem by granting a cor-
porate half life to the Jewish community. The Jewish community became, so to speak, the "family" to which all Jews
belonged. The role of the head of the family, exerting what
Roman law called *patria potestas* (paternal power), was transferred to the officials of the organized Jewish community.
These officials thus became the agents and deputies of the
rulers of the country. The relations of the Jewish community
to the larger group were often controlled by a special "Jewry
law." [7] The internal affairs of the Jewish groups were administered by the community officers, in accordance, wherever possible, with traditional Jewish law. In cases where
state legislation contradicted rabbinic law there was often an
attempt to find some way of compromising the conflict.
Moreover, as Salo W. Baron has pointed out, "Fiscal aspects
crept into these as into all other relations between the medieval states and their Jewries, the degree of Jewish judicial
autonomy frequently being determined by the revenue it
was likely to supply to a ruler." [8] Conflict and interference
between state law and Jewish law was, of course, less likely
to occur in the field of religious law than in civil or criminal
law. With the growing participation of Jews in the commercial life of the times and the increasing complexity and in-
volvement of mercantile matters, a very large number of suits
arising out of these activities came before Jewish courts, and
in these cases, needless to say, the possibilities of contradiction between Jewish law and state law were high.

Although basically the medieval Jewish community served

as a legal device to bring the Jews within the framework of status society, it had many other functions with regard to the inner life of the Jews. The officers of the community exerted control over most of the affairs of Jewish life. They were charged with the religious and educational leadership of the people. They maintained the ancient Jewish traditions of philanthropy and social welfare activity. Both the internal finances of the community and the just apportionment of the state taxes among the Jewish residents fell under the jurisdiction of the communal authorities. When subordinate agencies were needed for particular purposes, the officers of the community made the necessary decisions and authorized the inevitable expenditures. The Jewish communal organization was primary; all the other organizations of Jewish life—synagogues, cemeteries, schools, orphanages, almshouses, slaughterhouses, bakeshops, ritual baths—were secondary and depended for their existence and their maintenance upon the community. The professional functionaries of these secondary organizations—rabbis, teachers, ritual slaughterers, performers of the rite of circumcision—were employees of the community assigned by the community to their special tasks and responsibilities. The community and its officers had many important functions beside serving as a link between the Christian government and the Jews, helping to maintain the uneasy and often awkward situation in which the Jews were forced to live.

It is important for our purposes here to remember that, except in terms of the theology of the Christians, the situation was not of the Jews' own making. The Jews did not choose this way of life, nor yet could they avoid it. Yet this *modus vivendi,* which was certainly not developed with the interests of Jewish life in view, had many advantages for the Jews and for Judaism. It virtually guaranteed, even though this was not required by the express terms of the law, that all Jews would live in the same section of the town. In this way it reenforced the social compulsion on Jews to live as Jews. In a status society the alternative to living as a Jew was to become a Christian. The road of indifference was not open. Participation in the Jewish community gave the individual Jew a place in the world; nonparticipation was the equivalent of nonentity. In some cases, Jews against whom a communal ban was pronounced were subject to having their property confiscated by the civil ruler. Thus a tremendous power to enforce conformity was placed in the hands of the leaders of the Jewish communities. Under these circumstances, to live as a Jew meant to follow in every detail the traditional patterns of one's community. No individual could determine for himself what he would observe and what he would not, except at the risk of facing the disastrous ban. Any adjustments of the tradition to altered conditions, any allowances or modifications to meet a conflict of laws could be made only by the rabbinical leadership of the community, and such special ordinances (*takkanoth*) applied alike to all members of the community.

Special ordinances of this sort illustrate extremely well the normal relation of tradition and innovation as these two forces have operated within the Jewish religion. In every case in which a novel ordinance was adopted its enactment was reluctant and every possible mode of compromise was tried before the innovation was resorted to. In every case the new ordinance met a local situation and its permanence depended upon its continuing to satisfy the needs of the local situation. Over the centuries the minor adaptations thus introduced might add up to a considerable difference of pattern (*minhag*) between community and community. At no time, however, would the cumulative effect of new legislation be sufficiently great to break down the inner unity or sense of continuity within any single community. The changes introduced by small modifications of the over-all pattern were responses to minor shifts in the prevailing winds of the surrounding environment, not products of the tempests of crisis.[9]

STIRRINGS OF NEW LIFE

The appearance of stability and order in medieval society masked an underlying progressive character. Older students of the period were deceived by the surface calm and insisted on the description of medieval culture as static. More recently, perhaps, there has been an overcorrection of the error of the past, marked by the attempt to find the roots of all modern ideas in the middle ages. Certainly the intellectual life of the later middle ages was far more dynamic than its social life, and it is by no means possible any longer to assert a radical discontinuity between the thought of the middle ages and that of the Renaissance. Discontinuity was greatest in the social, political, and economic life of Europe, but even here the change took place far more gradually than the abruptness of historical periodization would suggest. Energies that had for centuries been directed to retarding the pincers thrust of Muslim expansionism into Europe could be redirected into more constructive channels as that thrust was turned back. The decimation of the population of Europe by the Black Plague of 1348 allowed, for the first time in centuries, more than a subsistence food level for those who remained alive.[10] Commerce, which had never disappeared completely, became an important element in the new dynamism that pervaded Europe.[11] The Holy Roman Empire, designed by the papacy to serve as the secular arm of the Church in the governing of Europe, became a mere shadow as modern secular states began to emerge. Urban civilization burst forth with renewed vigor after the pervasive ruralism of centuries. Universities, arts, and letters came alive and flourished under the spur of the vital stimulation flowing from the newer trends in European social life. The older "status" basis of society yielded place to a "contractual" basis emphasizing the talents and role of individuals. European society illustrates Maine's principle "that the movement of the progressive societies has hitherto been a movement *from Status to Contract.*" [12]

As the relatively stable medieval synthesis broke down and was reorganized in the various ways that have been suggested, the number and frequency of contacts between Jew and non-Jew increased. There were close business relationships, and close friendships, too, between some of the leading figures of the Renaissance, especially in Italy, and their Jewish associates. Some Jews even became frequenters of the papal court; during the reign of Pope Clement VII (1523–34), a member of the family of the Medici, two Jewish pseudo Messiahs, David Reubeni and Solomon Molcho, received papal hospitality, and the pope even protected Molcho against proceedings by the Inquisition.[13] Important churchmen, like Cardinal Egidio da Viterbo, and nobles, like Pico della Mirandola, devoted a substantial amount of time to Hebrew studies and entertained Jewish scholars.[14] In Venice, according to the testimony of Leon da Modena's letters, there was a group of rabbis and Christian ecclesiastics that met periodically for friendly discussions of religious subjects. Modena himself was sufficiently a man of his age to have written responses to queries from Christian correspondents concerning matters of Jewish religion; in at least one instance Modena's response was written in Latin.[15] Salomone de' Rossi is an excellent illustration of the participation of Jews in the artistic life of the times. He was attached for many years to the court of the duke of Mantua as a viol player; in addition to performing for the court he created a large number of original musical compositions that are still regarded as among the finest works of his period. Moreover he created for the use of synagogues liturgical music in which the sacred words of the psalms and the liturgy are set to characteristically Renaissance melodies.[16] In the early seventeenth century Rabbi Abraham Joseph Graziani of Modena went so far as to permit the use of the organ for synagogal music, despite the long-standing traditional view that all instrumental music was improper.[17] Thus the interpenetration of Jewish and Gentile culture in the world of the Renaissance is manifest.

Jews shared with Christians not only the finer and nobler aspects of Renaissance life; they shared its baser aspects, too. One of the distinguishing characteristics of the times was a widespread concern for personal adornment and for a luxurious way of life. Jews in the Renaissance also sought luxury. Another of the less attractive features of the age was its passion for gambling. Jewish religious tradition in the middle ages had explicitly attacked games of chance, although card games were then unknown to the Jews.[18] In the fifteenth century, however, Jews began to be caught up in the passion for card-playing; Cecil Roth gently suggests that the Jews' "spirit of adventure" was "partly diverted into such sordid channels." Whatever the reason, there are records of Jews losing as much as 3,000 ducats (approximately $6,900) in one session at cards.[19] Local Jewish communities went so far as to enact a ban of excommunication against inveterate card-players:

> During festivities at the court of Sardinia in Alghero, early in the fifteenth century, a well known Jewish gamester who was watching the gambling was ordered by the king to take a hand, notwithstanding the ban of excommunication which the local community had recently enacted against persons who indulged in the vice; and the rabbi, who happened to be present at the time (testimony, incidentally, to the degree of social emancipation enjoyed locally by the Jews), was sorely perplexed to know whether or not he was to be reckoned an offender.[20]

Even so distinguished a figure as Rabbi Leon da Modena could not resist the lure of cards, although as a youth he had written a tract condemning gambling. Time after time, despite firm resolutions and even solemn vows, Modena returned to the card tables, where he lost more than he could afford. When the Jewish community of Venice enacted an ordinance against gambling, Modena turned his great talents to the attempt to prove that this prohibition was contrary to Talmudic law.[21]

Although this evidence indicates frequent intimate relationships between Jews and Christians during the Renaissance, there is another side to the story. Despite the greater openness of society in the changed situation, some attempts were made to maintain the special place of the Jews as a group. Not until after the breakdown of the medieval synthesis was the designation of special streets of Jewish residence made a legal requirement in many places in Europe; the Jewish quarter from which the very name *ghetto* is derived was that of Venice, established only in 1516.[22] In part this is to be understood as a consequence of the passionate religious zeal that lay so close to the surface, the zeal of the "counter-Renaissance." As Roth acutely observed, "Savonarola was as much a son of the Italian Renaissance as Lorenzo de' Medici, and . . . the reforming movement associated with his name is as characteristic of the period and of the country as, let us say, the career of Cesare Borgia." [23] Every wave of religious revivalism was accompanied by a wave of violence directed against the Jews. In part, too, restrictions against the Jews as a group are intelligible as a response of "native" businessmen to Jewish competition or as an expression of lower-class resentment against pawnbrokers and moneylenders. But it is also important that we understand the contrast of an open situation for the individual Jew and restrictive regulation for the Jewish group as a feature of an age of transition from status to contract.

In the establishment of ghettos we may see an attempt to retain a status situation for the Jews after most of Europe had already largely transformed itself into a contract society. For one of the implications of contract society is that a man's place in the world is determined solely by his own achievements; it was on this basis that the place of the individual

Jew in Renaissance society was established. As we have seen, in status society a man's place is fixed by the nature of the group into which he happens to be born; this is the principle upon which general restrictions might be imposed upon the Jewish group. Even in the middle ages it was possible for a Jew of truly exceptional abilities to break through the chains of status and to achieve an independent, individual success, marked, perhaps, by a patent of nobility. In the Renaissance, despite all restrictions, more and more individual Jews were able to win their places in the world by their own talents. It was hardly reasonable to expect that in a society in upheaval, in which the general direction of social movement was toward individualism, in which traditional status patterns were everywhere tending toward disruption only the anomalous semi-status of the Jews would remain fixed. And it did not, despite restrictive laws.

Of all the countries of late Renaissance Europe, Holland maintained the fewest restrictions against the Jews. From Holland there came the move leading to the unofficial readmission of the Jews to England in the time of Oliver Cromwell. Even when, in Restoration times, Jews received official permission to settle in England, they were subject to restrictions of various types and were debarred from civil rights.[24] Some forms of trade were closed to them; the very title of a proposed parliamentary act in 1663 referred to the prevention of "Encroachments in Trade by the *Jews,* and *French,* and other Foreigners." [25] Not until the controversial and soon-repealed Naturalization Act of 1753 was any official attempt made to transfer individual English Jews from alien status to citizenship. Spain and Portugal had expelled their Jewish populations at the end of the fifteenth century; it is undoubtedly merely coincidental that the decline of the Iberian powers began soon thereafter. In Germany, as in Italy, the disunity of the country meant that interruptions to the stream of Jewish life and Jewish participation in the general life of the country were local and temporary. Persecutions were of frequent occurrence but of limited extent and duration; there was no general expulsion.

Meanwhile, in 1654, the first permanent Jewish settlers came to North America, to New York, then New Amsterdam, under the rule of the Dutch. They came to a land that had known no middle ages, that was a creature of the restless and adventurous dynamic individualism of the Renaissance. This handful of early Jewish settlers began an experiment whose conclusion is as yet unknown, an experiment of living as free men in a free land and still preserving, voluntarily, the institutions and customs of Judaism and of Jewish life. They did not have to be formally emancipated, these first American Jews, although, in some few instances, they had to struggle against restrictions imposed by custom. They are really the first modern Jews.

## ENLIGHTENMENT AND THE EMANCIPATION OF THE JEWS

Even though the Jews were never as fully excluded from the life of their times in Europe as the usual oversimplified historical account would suggest, there was surely an increasing participation of individual Jews in the intellectual, social, and political life of Europe from the fourteenth through the seventeenth centuries, the period called the Renaissance. From time to time the Western nations recognized and rewarded the special services of individual Jews by granting them citizenship and political rights. For the vast majority of the Jews of Europe, however, political participation was impossible. Everywhere the Jews were regarded as foreigners, as resident aliens, rather than as citizens. The laws under which Jews lived differed from those under which other residents of the same lands lived. They had, through the Jewish self-governing communities, a government of their own, instead of being directly and immediately subject to the rule of the sovereign of the country in which they lived. As a result the religion of Judaism was not subject to radical and extreme stresses. For only radical and extreme changes in environing conditions demand the complete rethinking of a religious tradition.

In the meantime, however, intellectual, social, and political forces that had begun in the late middle ages and had gathered momentum during the Renaissance came to a focus in the late seventeenth and eighteenth centuries to create a short-lived but important age of enlightenment. Its basic ideas were few and simple: The universe is an orderly and rational collection of things whose relations are governed by law. The mind of man is an instrument by means of which he can penetrate the secrets of the universe; man's rationality is adequate to the discovery of the rationale of the universe; man, therefore, needs no reliance upon supernatural revelation or other sources of authority as guides to his life in the universe. Granted that the operations of the human mind are not perfect; it is enough that they are perfectible. Granted that men make mistakes; it is enough that they are corrigible.

The intelligent world is far from being so well governed as the physical. For though the former has also its laws, which of their own nature are invariable, it does not conform to them so exactly as the physical world. This is because, on the one hand, particular intelligent beings are of a finite nature, and consequently liable to error; and on the other, their nature requires them to be free agents. Hence they do not steadily conform to their primitive laws; and even those of their own instituting they frequently infringe.[26]

In most men, most of the time, reason is an adequate guide in all affairs. Not only is this true of personal affairs; it holds also for political, economic, and religious matters. An enlightened age requires only that men have the courage to release themselves from bondage to authority:

Enlightenment is man's release from self-imposed tutelage. Tutelage is the inability to use one's natural powers without direction from another. This tutelage is called "self-imposed" because its cause is not any absence of rational competence but simply a lack of courage and resolution to use one's reason without direction from another. . . . Religious tutelage is not only the most harmful but the most degrading of all.[27]

Such faith in human reason and human reasonableness may seem to twentieth-century man incredibly naive. In its own time, however, it was a clarion call to freedom and to respect for one's fellow man as a being of rationality comparable to one's own.

To an enlightened mind the differences between men that had been stressed by thinkers of earlier times were of no great significance. Certainly to those who were skeptical of the doctrines of Christianity, except where they could be reached by reason, differences of religion were of no consequence whatsoever for secular life. If men's political decisions were to be made by the reasoned judgments of members of the political community, their religious affiliations were completely irrelevant to these decisions. If economic decisions were to be based upon each man's reasoned conclusions of his own ultimate self-interest, questions of religious affiliation were completely inconsequential. If social intercourse were to be grounded upon the possibility of improving one's own use of reason by association and conversation with men of comparable intellectual stature, then surely differences of religion between friends were completely immaterial to their association. The tolerant acceptance of individual Jews in the courts of the Italian Renaissance was followed by the warm welcome of individual Jewish intellectuals to the salons of the Enlightenment.[28]

In the British colonies in North America the ideas of the Enlightenment were more than an intellectual fad. Partly because of the need for justification of the colonial position at the time of the Revolution and partly because of the germ of an enlightened attitude that inhered in the most widely accepted forms of American Protestantism, a philosophy of Enlightenment was so generally accepted in America that it could be made the foundation of the claim to political independence. The Declaration of Independence, Jefferson's Act to Establish Religious Freedom in Virginia, the Constitution of the United States of America, and the Bill of Rights—the primary documents of American nationhood—are all expressions of an enlightened view of man and the universe. Because of the prevalence of the ideas of the Enlightenment as well as because of the absence of a heritage of restriction, it was readily possible in most of the American colonies for Jews to attain full citizenship, full participation in the political life of the country as well as in all other aspects of life. To my mind, it is most revealing that there were Jewish civil servants in the administration of President Washington; that a Jew was a member of the very first entering class when the United States Military Academy was established; and that a special table providing *kosher* refreshments was set up for the Philadelphia parade celebrating the adoption of the Constitution in 1789.[29]

The European Enlightenment did not start with a clean slate. The proscriptions and restrictions of centuries hampered the *illuminati* of Europe and made it difficult for them to put into public practice their belief in the equality of all men, including Jews. In their private lives they did what they pleased. But when, toward the end of the eighteenth century, the idea of political emancipation for the Jews of Western Europe began to be bruited about, there were two models at hand. One was the gradual entry of the Jews into all other aspects of European life. The other was the full entry of the Jews into the political life of the United States of America. Political emancipation came to the Jews of Western Europe as a by-product of the French Revolution and the Napoleonic conquests. This was a historic accident; the emancipation would have come in any case as a consequence of the spirit of the age, the *Zeitgeist* of Enlightenment.

MOSES MENDELSSOHN AND HIS CIRCLE

Even before emancipation there were Jews who accepted to the full the invitation to Enlightenment that pervaded advanced intellectual circles in the eighteenth century The most notable of the Jewish *illuminati* was Moses Mendelssohn (1729–1786), friend of the poet-playwright, Gotthold Lessing, and associate of the greatest philosopher of the Enlightenment, Immanuel Kant.[30] Mendelssohn was born in the ghetto of Dessau and from early youth revealed an acute mind and a passion for study. By the time he was fourteen years of age he had mastered the Talmud and the major rabbinical texts, under the tutelage of Rabbi David Fränkel. When his teacher left Dessau for Berlin, in 1743, Mendelssohn followed him to the metropolis. In Berlin the young Jewish scholar found employment to sustain his body while he pursued studies in modern languages, mathematics, and the secular sciences to sustain his spirit. Lessing and Mendelssohn met over a game of chess and became fast friends; as a consequence of this friendship Mendelssohn was introduced into the literary circles of his time. But his reputation was firmly established when, in 1763, he won a prize given by the Prussian Academy of Sciences, for an essay on a metaphysical subject, over two competitors, one of whom was Immanuel Kant.

Mendelssohn's success in this competition, his mastery of an excellent German style, and a volume of his philosophical discourses, published with the connivance of Lessing and without the author's knowledge, placed him on a pinnacle. His essays and articles were sought by the leading journals; the Prussian government granted him the status of "Protected Jew" (*Schutzjude*); he became a celebrity. Yet, in spite of his success in the larger literary and social world, Moses Mendelssohn faithfully adhered to the practices of Judaism. This was not a matter of display or advertisement but of deep attachment to tradition. He was firmly convinced that other

Jews could, as he had done, become masters of both traditional Jewish learning and modern secular knowledge. A considerable part of his literary effort was devoted to the attempt to make this double achievement possible. In this respect his most important single monument was a translation of the Pentateuch into German, for the use of his fellow Jews, with a commentary written in Hebrew. Both parts were significant; the translation is the earliest major work of Jewish cultural life to be written in German, while the commentary goes beyond the traditional lines of rabbinic and talmudic discussion to introduce modern concepts and modern approaches to the biblical text.

Properly, Mendelssohn's activities should be described as mediatorial: he tried to bring German culture to the Jews and to exemplify Jewish culture to the Germans. One of the ways in which he helped to make Jews aware of German culture was by establishing a literary periodical in Hebrew, *ha-Meassef* (The gatherer). The Jewish Free School, started in Berlin in 1781, and later imitated in other parts of the country, was another venture in Mendelssohnian mediation. Instruction comprehended both traditional and modern subjects, but all teaching was carried on in German. He tried consistently to open new horizons to the view of his fellow Jews. He even hired the brilliant *picaro,* Solomon Maimon, to translate important German works into Hebrew for the enlightenment of the Polish Jews.[31] As ambassador without portfolio of the Jews to the German people, Mendelssohn's original philosophical works, by virtue of which he was known to his contemporaries as "the Jewish Socrates," are important, but they should probably be ranked second to his now almost forgotten treatise, *Jerusalem* (1783), in which he argued the case for a separation of church and state in order that each may be able better to fulfil the functions for which it is ordained, and in order that freedom of thought may be permitted to men. In the second part of his treatise he interpreted Judaism through the glass of Enlightenment as revealed law but not revealed religion. The doctrines and historical truths associated with Judaism are not part of its unique revelation, but are available to all men through reason. Only the ceremonial law is unique to Judaism, and the ceremonial law tells the Jew not what to believe, but what to do.

I recognize no other eternal truths than those comprehensible to human reason and those provable and demonstrable through the human power to think. However, anyone who believes that I could not make such a claim without deviating from the religion of my ancestors is misled by a false concept of Judaism. On the contrary, I hold this to be an essential point in the Jewish religion, and I believe that this doctrine represents a characteristic difference between the Jewish and Christian faiths. To put it briefly: I believe that Judaism recognizes no revealed religion in the sense understood by Christians. The Israelites have divine legislation, laws, commandments, ordinances, rules of life, and instruction in the will of God concerning rules of conduct which are intended to lead to earthly as well as eternal salvation. These tenets and precepts have been revealed to them by Moses in a wonderful, supernatural way; but they are neither dogmas, nor redemptive truths, nor universal propositions demonstrable by reason. At all times, these latter truths are revealed to us and to all other humans by the Eternal, by nature, and by circumstance, but never by word or writing.[32]

The consequence of this view is that it is obligatory for the Jew to accept and conform to the ceremonial law, both as it is given in the Bible and as it is developed in the Talmud. This obligation is not a matter of reason. There is, however, no dogma, no creed, no belief that carries with it the same binding quality. Beliefs must be held on the ground of reason. Because he found himself able to justify rationally a belief in immortality, and did so to great applause in his dialogue, *Phaidon*, he held to this belief: [33] because he found himself unable to justify a belief in miracles, he abandoned this belief.

Among the immediate disciples of Mendelssohn the Hebrew poet Naphtali Herz Wessely (1725–1805) was important both for his literary creations and for his role in the diffusion of Mendelssohn's ideas on modern Jewish education. At first his writings were well received by the more traditional groups in Germany. Later, his constant call for extending the intellectual scope of Jewish education by a concern for the modern disciplines, and even for the application of these modern disciplines to traditional subjects, soon lost him the support of those who could not agree with his contention that the Jews themselves must bear some of the responsibility for their backwardness. Wessely admitted that the larger share of the blame for the poor state of Jewish education had to be assigned to those who had for so long excluded the Jew from advanced Western culture. But he insisted that it was the Jew's own responsibility to reawaken his slumbering intellect and to strive energetically to achieve knowledge.[34]

The stress of Mendelssohn and Wessely on education persisted into the nineteenth century. Both in Germany and in Poland the vision of an enlightened Jewry remained vivid long after the European Enlightenment had passed into history. Journals like *Sulamith* (in German with occasional Hebrew contributions, published irregularly from 1806 to 1840) clearly evince their Mendelssohnian inspiration.

*Sulamith* desires to arouse the [Jewish] nation to a respect of religion, that is, of those truths which alone are worthy of the name religion. It wants to revitalize the urgent need for religious sentiment and concepts, but at the same time it wants to point up the truth that the concepts and commands contained in the Jewish religion are in no wise harmful, either to the individual or to society. Further, it desires to bring the Jewish nation back to its native level of education. . . . *It wants to enlighten the Jewish nation about itself.*[35]

In one of its issues *Sulamith* contained a translation of information collected by Hannah Adams about the Jews of the United States.[36] Again the interest of enlightened Europe in the American scene is manifest.

OUT OF THE GHETTO, INTO THE WORLD

Mendelssohn's interpretation of Judaism and his success in living both as a pious follower of Jewish customs and as a citizen of the enlightened German world, as well as the conditions of the times, led to willing attention to suggestions for the civil emancipation of the Jews. Some early positive steps in the direction of full emancipation were taken by Emperor Joseph II of Austria, without much practical success, since the Jews did not respond as had been hoped to the relaxation of some of the discriminatory laws and to the external pressure to modernize, to Westernize, and ultimately to assimilate. The emperor eliminated some of the special taxes that had been imposed upon the Jews centuries earlier and abolished the regulation requiring each Jew to wear a distinctive badge advertising his ethnic status. Joseph II believed that emancipation should be a gradual process; step by step the public authorities were to ease or abrogate Jewish disabilities, and for each concession made by the authorities the Jews were to take a corresponding step toward merging themselves in the Austrian population. Thus, on the one hand, economic activities that had been closed to the Jews for centuries were opened to them, as were the publicly supported schools. On the other hand, by express edict, the Jews were ordered to follow the Western pattern by adopting distinctive surnames, instead of continuing the biblical custom of being known by their given names and those of their fathers. It had been by a voluntary change of this sort that Moses, the son of Mendel (Moses ben Mendel), translated his name as Moses Mendelssohn; now the law required that every Jew make such a change. Those who did not comply willingly and rapidly by registering their newly selected names with the authorities were given arbitrary, ridiculous, sometimes obscene names by order of the special commission. The concessions to Jewish emancipation that the emperor was prepared to make came at too high a cost for the Jews to accept them gladly.[37]

As early as the 1780s there was interest in Central Europe in what was taking place in the new United States. Although several of the state governments carried over from their colonial charters certain civil limitations on the Jews, the federal government, from the outset, had no restrictions. Neither the Articles of Confederation, under which the federal government operated until 1789, nor the Constitution which replaced the Articles made any distinction among citizens on grounds of religion. The Constitution specifically outlawed any test oath for any public office; the form prescribed for the presidential oath was so phrased that even a nonbeliever in any religion could conscientiously subscribe to it; the Articles of Confederation contained no reference to religion. This is well known today; what is less familiar is that even the details of discussions of religious matters in the Continental Congress were followed closely by Europeans. Thus we find Moses Mendelssohn, on the final page of his *Jerusalem*, expressing his sorrow that the Continental Congress had begun to "sing the old song" by discussing an establishment of religion.[38] It is hard for us to recapture the sense of new departure that attended the birth of the United States.

These preliminary indications of concern for Jewish emancipation, however, might have taken many years longer to produce results if it had not been for the overwhelming effect of the French Revolution. Not only the Jews of France, but also some of their non-Jewish sympathizers, notably the radical Churchman, Abbé Henri Grégoire,[39] recognized that the Declaration of the Rights of Man and of the Citizen (1789) provided a framework for the emancipation of the Jews.

I. Men are born, and always continue, free and equal in respect of their rights. Civil distinctions, therefore, can be founded only on public utility.
II. The end of all political associations is the preservation of the natural and imprescriptible rights of man; and these rights are

liberty, property, security, and resistance of oppression. . . .
X. No man ought to be molested on account of his opinions, not
even on account of his *religious* opinions, provided his avowal
of them does not disturb the public order established by the
law.[40]

After agitation by some of the Jews of Paris, fifty-three of
the sixty districts into which the revolutionary Paris Com-
mune was divided voted in favor of following the logic of the
Declaration of the Rights of Man by granting full citizenship
to the Jews of France. The National Assembly, after some
delay, passed a motion enfranchising the Jews by an almost
unanimous vote, on September 27, 1791.[41] The soil had been
prepared elsewhere, but it was in revolutionary France that
the seed took root.

Thereafter emancipation began by following the military
successes of the French and ultimately had to be accepted
even where the French armies were not victorious. In 1796
the scene was Holland, where the National Assembly voted
emancipation after an extended debate, in which the American experience was referred to by two of the participants
(one on each side of the question), and pressure by the French
representative; in 1797 Jews were elected to the Dutch legisla-
ture. In Italy, still disunited, each separate kingdom had to
act separately on Jewish emancipation, starting with Venice,
in 1797. Disunited Germany reveals a pattern similar to that
of Italy, appearing, except in the Rhineland, a decade later.
It is of interest to note here that in Prussia, where Jewish
emancipation came in 1812, the civil service remained closed
to Jews.[42]

Emancipation inspired by the French Revolution ended
with the reaction of 1815. Only Holland and France retained
full civil rights for Jews. But during the nineteenth century
emancipated status returned in country after country until,
by the 1870s, all the Jews of Western Europe were free from
the galling bonds of statutory restriction. Emancipation had
finally come to the Jews with the recognition that differences

of religious belief and affiliation offered no obstacle to their full and loyal participation in the political, social, and economic life of their countries. Nineteenth-century liberal nationalism finally broke down the barriers that Renaissance individualism and Enlightenment rational humanitarianism had weakened. The Jews finally were permitted to come out of the ghetto and into the world.

THE WORLD INTO WHICH THEY ENTERED

Since the end of the eighteenth century, then, in one country of Western Europe after another, the official disposition of the people and the rulers has been to regard Jews as citizens of a different faith from that of the majority of their fellow citizens. From time to time, of course, there has been a resurgence of medieval attitudes among leaders, and the reluctance of some participants in the Roman Catholic Church's ecumenical council (Vatican II) to enact a revised schema concerning relations between Christians and Jews is evidence that older theological distinctions are not yet dead. Social relations are still, as they properly should be, largely matters of personal preference, but as the public opportunities for more frequent contact between Jews and Christians increase in number a personal preference across religious lines is more probable. In short, the past century and a half has been marked by a bridging of the ancient gap between the Jew and his neighbor.

The older way, the way of segregation, had its problems, some of which have been referred to here. The new order, the emancipated order, has created new problems. One to which attention should be called is that of the "hyphenated Jew"—the German-Jew, the French-Jew, the English-Jew, the American-Jew. In the earlier periods, when the Jews lived perforce in a community apart, it was unlikely that any conflict would arise between their loyalties. The Jew who lived in France or Germany knew himself to be a Jew permitted to live in France or in Germany. No circumstance could put him in the intolerable position of trying to decide whether his first loyalty was to France or Germany, or whether it was to Judaism. As far as France or Germany was concerned, he knew himself to be a barely tolerated outsider. The hyphenated Jew is forever confronted with precisely this sort of decision. There is scarcely a major issue with respect to which he does not need to decide whether his primary loyalty lies with the Jewish roots of his being or with the country into which he has been, as it were, adopted. With good fortune there may be few occasions on which the two loyalties come into sharp conflict, but think, for example, of what it must have meant to be a French-Jew at the time of the Dreyfus Affair, or a German-Jew under the Hitler regime. Or, to bring this closer to home, think of the American-Jew trying to decide whether the need of the United States for Middle Eastern oil outweighs, in his personal scale of values, the inevitable damage to the Jewish state in Israel that will follow on the strengthening of the Middle Eastern states by American money and American technology.

A less heart-rending but no less important issue is raised for the Jews by the basically secular nature of modern life. It was, in the first instance, the increasing secularization of the idea of the nation that, combined with other features that have been noted, made possible the emancipation of the Jews. If, in the eighteenth and nineteenth centuries, religion had still been regarded as a primary bond of national unity, the emancipation of the Jews, being the entry and acceptance of members of a different religious group into the nation, could not have occurred. By the end of the eighteenth century, however, geographic contiguity and economic community had replaced religion as central to the idea of the nation. Jewish emancipation was, in part, a product of the secularization of modern life.

What does it mean to say that the modern age is a secular age? On the surface, the most obvious meaning is that "worldly" rather than religious activities occupy a central place in the lives of people. When the concept of secularization is defined in this way, the definition is more Christian than Jewish, because the distinction between religious life and worldly life has been less prominent in Jewish than in Christian thought. The nature of secularization becomes clearer if we consider it as one of the chief factors in the compartmentalizing of life. The life of the individual is not regarded as a unity, in which religious motivations are central; instead, each aspect of his life is, so to speak, filed away in a separate compartment. His family life goes into one box, his business or professional life into another, his social activities into a third, his religion into a fourth, and so on. Each of the areas into which a man's life is pieced has its own motivations, its own rationale, its own set of rules. He tries, consciously, to prevent the spilling over of ideas from one phase of life into another; and no wonder, for disaster could come from allowing the ideas of religion to creep into our ways of doing business—and still worse disaster from permitting our ways of doing business to influence our religion. More importantly, secularization means that modern man is unable to avail himself of any single, unifying principle of explanation, such as the one permitted our ancestors by the concepts of God's will and God's providence. Each compartmentalized fragment of life has its own appropriate type of explanation.

Now, if modern life is divided in this fashion, and if the compartment that contains a man's religion is just one box among many, and if this box is the only one in which a man differs significantly from other members of his society, it will not be long before he will question the need and the desirability of maintaining this distinctness. Not all men will answer the question in the same way. What is important for our purposes here is that it is a major question. It is a critical question. This question cannot be answered by making minor adjustments or new ordinances, but only by a reconsideration of the roots of our beliefs. For if our religious beliefs cannot retain their relevance as guides to life here and now, they can no longer hold our loyalty and devotion. Each of the world's major faiths has been faced with a crisis since the birth of the modern world, and each of the faiths has, in its own special way, made efforts to meet the crisis of modernity with its concomitant of secularization. The nineteenth and twentieth centuries rank with the greatest periods of religious creativity precisely because all religions must come to terms with the modern age or die.

Modern Judaism has, however, faced an especially severe crisis because its radical quest for new terms in which to meet the new world was twinborn with the emancipation of the Jews. Judaism was able to meet and to survive earlier challenges, in part, at least, because of the cohesiveness of the Jewish group, externally manifested in the institution of the Jewish community. As a by-product of emancipation, the *raison d'être* of the Jewish community disappeared. Full citizens of modern Western states needed no structure to stand between them and their governments. Thus emancipation weakened Jewish group life. It destroyed almost completely the viability of the Jewish community, which survived, where it did survive at all, as a vestigial organ with no remaining function. At the same time, emancipation certainly strengthened the position of individual Jews, making it possible for the outstanding among them to take a place on the world stage that would otherwise have been denied them because they were Jews, increasing the opportunities of smaller local success for the less outstanding, and making life more tolerable and less hazardous for all the rest.

The critical problem that has been faced by modern Judaism has been that of retaining the benefits of emancipation without being swept under by its disadvantages while, at the same time, reformulating its theology and adapting its practices to the secular character of the modern world. Various answers to this problem have been suggested and several of these answers are being tested in the crucible of experimental verification through alternative forms of Jewish institutional life. The Reform, Conservative, and Orthodox movements of modern times, and in many ways the Zionist movement, are to be understood as tentative instruments of this verification process; these movements are all movements *within* Jewish life. Assimilation to the surrounding population is another answer that has been tested during this period of adjustment; it is a way that may completely satisfy the individual who assimilates, but that cannot satisfy the group's need for an answer that preserves Judaism. There are other answers, too, that, like assimilation, will not concern us here. We shall examine the major proposals and see how far each of them answers the need for a relevant revision of traditional Judaism and a guide to Jews living emancipated lives in the modern world.

Moses Mendelssohn had no difficulty in proposing a general principle to direct the behavior of emancipated Jews. "Comply," he wrote, "with the customs and the civil constitutions of the countries in which you are transplanted, but, at the same time, be constant to the faith of your forefathers." [43] This principle could readily be accepted by proponents of all the modern varieties of Judaism, but it is a principle far easier to formulate than to implement. With only the slightest exaggeration, it might be said that the whole course of Jewish thought and Jewish institutional development from the time of Mendelssohn to our own days has been a series of commentaries on this sentence. The discussion has centered more on how to be constant to the faith of the forefathers than on how to comply with the customs and civil constitutions of the various Western countries. It is one characteristic of modern Judaism in all its varieties that constancy to the ancestral faith has been more of a problem than has adaptation to the surrounding world.

The first attempt to develop a modernized form of Judaism came in the Reform movement, to which we shall turn our attention in the next chapter.

# 2

# The Initial Response: Reform Judaism in Europe and America

## THE WESTERNIZATION OF JUDAISM

During the middle ages one of the techniques instituted in the hope of converting the Jews to Christianity was the imposition of a requirement that all adult Jewish males attend a special church service two or three times a year. At this conversion service a noted revival preacher would hold forth for at least two hours. An official was appointed to make sure that the Jewish audience stayed awake during the long harangue.[1] Needless to say, this forced attendance did not lead to any desire on the part of the Jews to bring Jewish services into accord with what they saw of Christian services. During the Renaissance, however, when a number of Jews, even of rabbis, voluntarily attended Christian religious services, especially in Italy, many began to be dissatisfied with the esthetic deficiencies of synagogue services.[2] Jewish services were inordinately long; the original brief prayer service and reading from the Torah had been amplified by the inclusion of a large number of medieval religious poems (*piyyutim*), chanted to melodies that seemed to the more cultured ears of Renaissance men orientally barbaric. By long-standing custom there was no instrumental music, although the Bible reports the use of instrumental music in the Temple at Jerusalem.[3] As a result of this esthetic dissatisfaction with the synagogue service, attempts were made, during the Italian Renaissance, to modernize and Europeanize, or Westernize, synagogal music and liturgy. This is the context for Salomone de' Rossi's liturgical music and for the introduction of an organ in the Mantuan synagogue. Roth also reports on the use of popular songs of the period as settings for psalms and hymns, and quotes Judah Moscato's protest: "What shall we say and how shall we justify ourselves as regards some of the synagogue cantors of our day, who chant the holy prayers to the tunes of popular songs of the multitude, and thus, while they are discoursing on holy themes, think of the original ignoble and licentious association." [4]

The early start toward a Westernization of the synagogue service had no effect in the synagogues of Germany. Furthermore, because traditional Judaism had isolated itself in the sixteenth and seventeenth centuries, in response to the segregation of the Jews by the civil authorities, the synagogue services had become even more unappealing to those Jews who had moved out into the world under the spur of Enlightenment. The ancient institution of preaching had deteriorated to the point where an exposition of rabbinic law might take the place of a sermon, and even these legalistic discourses were delivered only twice a year. The traditional language of the synagogue was Hebrew; but for prayers in Hebrew to be meaningful to the worshipers, they had to be understood, and the teaching of Hebrew in the Jewish schools of Germany had decayed into a rote memorization of the words of the prayers without any concern for their meaning. To enlightened Jews in the late eighteenth and early nineteenth centuries the services as conducted in the synagogues were intolerable.[5]

The educational efforts of Moses Mendelssohn were, in part, directed toward eliminating one side of this difficulty. His program called for a much more effective mode of teaching Hebrew, in order that the prayers and the Bible when read or recited in Hebrew might be intelligible to the participants. In this connection it must be recalled that Mendelssohn was a firm traditionalist with respect to the maintenance of the ceremonial law. He did not want to change the synagogue service, but to change the worshipers.[6] Some of his followers had no such reservation. Their growing awareness of the currents of rationality in Western thought led, as a secondary effect, to the demand that Judaism itself be Westernized. David Friedländer (1756–1834) was one of the first of the Mendelssohnians to voice this demand, in his *Sendschreiben an . . . Probst Teller,* 1799 (Letters to Councilman Teller). Here he declared:

From century to century these prayers became more and more numerous and worse and worse, the conceptions more mystical, muddied with the principles of kabbala which were in direct contradiction to the genuine spirit of Judaism. And finally, the language in which these prayers are expressed not only offends the ear, but also mocks at all language and grammar. The larger portion of our nation understands nothing of these prayers and that is a happy circumstance, because in this way these prayers will have neither good nor bad effect on the sentiment of the worshippers.[7]

Friedländer's complaints were not unique. As early as 1796, in Amsterdam, Holland, a new synagogue, Adath Jeshurun, was organized for the express purpose of introducing reforms. The agitation attending its formation was considerable, and yet the reforms of the service that took place were very minor: some of the religious poetry of the middle ages was omitted, and the delivery of public addresses in Dutch was allowed.[8]

Liturgical reform was certainly not a great issue, but it was the issue on which conflict between the traditionalists and the innovators, in the early nineteenth century, was joined. Scholarship among the adherents of the rabbinical tradition as well as in the general Jewish population was neither profound nor extensive. Neither the rabbis nor the laity had the competence to carry on any adequate debate concerning the basic principles of the Jewish faith. Under these circumstances the dissatisfaction of the more enlightened among the people expressed itself in resentment of the "oriental" elements in the worship of the synagogue and in the desire that the traditional ritual be purged, so that Jewish services could achieve the dignity and decorum of Protestant Christian worship. Each proposal for modification of the service met with bitter resistance, the traditionalist party going so far, in several instances, as to appeal successfully to the secular government to support its authority against those who would introduce modifications of the forms of worship.

Because the opposition of followers of the traditional pattern made the establishment of new synagogues difficult, if not impossible, the first significant steps toward the development of a Reform movement in Judaism took place in the schools set up by the followers of Mendelssohn. Modifications could be introduced into the services carried on for the students in these schools, and justified on the ground of the youth and lack of knowledge of the pupils. These young people, however, when they grew to maturity, had become accustomed to changes that would have stirred spirited protest in their parents, and they provided the popular base of German Reform Judaism. Perhaps these factors explain the delay in the institutionalization of German Reform; the initial impulse preceded the formal establishment of Reformed synagogues by from ten to fifteen years. Israel Jacobson (1768–1828) of Seesen, in Central Germany, deserves special mention in this connection.[9] He was a successful and wealthy businessman, not a scholar, and he was deeply attached to Judaism. It disturbed him to note the degree to which the more cultured German Jews were alienated from

Judaism, and he attributed their self-alienation to the lifeless ceremonialism of the religion. As a practical man he sought to find a way in which the synagogue could be revitalized so that, without losing its hold on the uneducated masses, it might regain the interest of the enlightened Jews.

The Napoleonic conquest of western Germany gave Jacobson the opportunity to try out some of his ideas, for he was appointed president of the Jewish consistory of Westphalia, the official body created for the direction of all Jewish affairs. Jacobson had earlier instituted a Jewish school at Seesen; now, in Cassel, the governing seat of his consistory, Jacobson established another school. Here services of worship were held each Saturday, and at these services German was used for some of the prayers, hymns in German were sung by a school choir, and a weekly sermon was delivered, again in German, by one of the members of the consistory. These innovations were so well received, meeting so little opposition, that Jacobson decided to go farther; he paid entirely out of his own pocket for the building of a new synagogue at Seesen, included an organ as part of its equipment, and trained the choir of the school at Seesen to participate in the services. The dedication ceremonies, on July 17, 1810, provided the occasion for a tremendous amount of adulation and congratulation, and have even been described, in German-Jewish sources, as the Festival of the Jewish Reformation.[10] Jacobson himself delivered the dedicatory address, in which the emphasis on ritual reform stands out:

Who would dare to deny that our service is sickly because of many useless things, that in part it has degenerated into a thoughtless recitation of prayers and formulae, that it kills devotion more than encourages it, and that it limits our religious principles to that fund of knowledge which for centuries has remained in our treasure houses without increase and without ennoblement. On all sides, enlightenment opens up new areas for development. Why should we alone remain behind? [11]

After this first venture in 1810 there were abortive attempts to set up Reform synagogues in Berlin in 1815, and finally a triumph, marking the true beginning of Reform Judaism as an organized and institutionalized religious movement, in the building and dedication of the Hamburg Temple in 1818.

Eduard Kley (1789–1867), who was one of the moving spirits in the foundation of the Hamburg Temple,[12] had earlier been involved in the unsuccessful effort to introduce Reform Judaism in Berlin, and with one of his Berlin colleagues, Karl Siegfried Günsburg (1788–1860), had produced, in 1817, the first Jewish prayer book entirely in the German language.[13] Two of the other leaders of the Hamburg Temple, Meyer Israel Bresselau (1785–1839) and Seckel Isaak Fränkel (1765–1835), edited the prayer book (1819) for the new Temple.[14] Since there was so much concern for ritual reform among the leaders, it is not surprising that the constitution of the founding group emphasized the Westernization of worship:

Since public worship has for some time been neglected by so many, because of the ever decreasing knowledge of the language in which alone it has until now been conducted, and also because of many other shortcomings which have crept in at the same time—the undersigned, convinced of the necessity to restore public worship to its deserving dignity and importance, have joined together . . . to arrange . . . a dignified and well-ordered ritual according to which the worship service shall be conducted.[15]

Among the innovations the constitution specifically refers to the introduction of "a German sermon, and choral singing to the accompaniment of an organ." [16]

When the party of tradition mounted a full-scale attack on the Hamburg Temple the limitations of the Reform movement of those early days became woefully clear. Reform Judaism lacked a philosophical groundwork to justify its ritual changes, and it lacked a sufficient historical and critical knowledge of the very tradition it was trying to revitalize. In time both these deficiencies were to be eliminated; in the 1840s Reform Judaism developed an adequate and comprehensive philosophy, while even earlier a group of young and dedicated scholars, largely motivated by reformist impulses, had brought to birth the scientific study (*Wissenschaft*) of Judaism.

## THE INTELLECTUAL MATURATION OF REFORM JUDAISM

In 1819 a group of about fifty young men banded together in Berlin to give organized expression to a new and significant concept: that Judaism and its history, its literature, its cultural monuments, and its social matrix could be studied objectively and critically, yet sympathetically, in the manner of university studies. They called their organization *Verein für Kultur und Wissenschaft des Judenthums* (Society for Jewish culture and its scientific study). Their program was vast and ambitious; their actual achievements as a group were quite limited. Nevertheless, they succeeded in publishing one volume of a *Zeitschrift für die Wissenschaft des Judenthums* (Journal for the scientific study of Judaism) in 1822,[17] and in inspiring several major works of Jewish scholarship. Some of the participants in the work of the organized group retained the original emphasis on objectivity, even, as in the case of Isaak Markus Jost (1793–1860), to a fault. Others, more deeply committed to the Reform cause, deliberately exercised their scholarship for partisan purposes.[18] Yet in many ways the most important contribution of the scientific study of Judaism to Reform came about through the work of Leopold Zunz (1794–1886), who was most careful to keep himself unentangled in the religious controversies, dedicating himself exclusively to the material of his studies.

In 1817 when, at the request of the traditional party in Berlin, the government of Prussia had intervened to forbid the continuation of the "private" Reform congregation there, Zunz had been one of its preachers. The excuse given by the government for its action was that Judaism, since the birth of Christianity, was a mere survival, without life or the vigor to develop new patterns; the innovations proposed by the Reform group fell under this odd ban. Zunz then decided to study the question whether preaching and prayers in the local vernacular were in fact innovations in the Jewish tradition. He succeeded in proving that sermonic interpretations of the Bible in the vernacular had long been the custom in many Jewish communities, that literary and religious creativity had been perennially alive in Judaism, so that it had continued through the ages to produce new ideas and new patterns of expression appropriate to the time and place of their development. Zunz's study, *Die gottesdienstlichen Vorträge der Juden, historisch entwickelt* (The historical development of the Jewish sermon), published in 1832, was certainly the first and perhaps the greatest of the products of the application of academic criteria to the study of Jewish subject matter in the nineteenth century, and its conclusions buttressed the position of Reform Judaism.[19]

The philosophical underpinning of the early practical Reform movement in Germany was the great accomplishment of a generation of thinkers, many of whom began their careers as participants in the *Wissenschaft des Judenthums* group. Although these Reform philosophers of Judaism differed in detail among themselves, their impact as a group was to do for Western Jews and Westernized Judaism of the nineteenth century what Moses Maimonides had done for the Jews and the Judaism of the middle ages, to found an interpretation of Judaism on the most advanced philosophies of their age. Thus Solomon Ludwig Steinheim (1790–1866) based his large book, *Die Offenbarung nach dem Lehrbegriff der Synagoge* (Revelation according to the doctrinal system of the synagogue), published in 1835, on a critical version of the philosophy of Immanuel Kant. Steinheim followed the general line of the Kantian argument in examining the limits of the competence of human reason. Beyond the scope of reason, however, where Kant looked to intuition as a guide, Steinheim turned to revelation. Beyond the knowledge that men could gain by the use of their reason there lay, accord-

ing to Steinheim, a realm of supernatural knowledge be-
stowed upon men by divine grace. Steinheim differed from
Kant also in his manner of formulating the central principle
of ethics. Kant had argued that the moral life of man is
founded on the categorical demand of reason for universality.
Steinheim regarded this as far too formal and rigid. He suggested instead an idea frequently found in Jewish ethical
literature, that the moral life is the voluntary service that a
free man gives to his God. Then, most interestingly, Steinheim tied together these two points of his greatest divergence from Kant: Revelation is the Divine Word given to
man, but it was not given all at one time or at one place.
Some was given to the ancients and is reported in the Bible,
along with much else that is not genuine revelation. Which
part of the biblical revelation is genuine can be discovered
only by an act of faith. The living evidence of this act of
faith is the voluntary adherence to the moral life.[20]

Whether it was Steinheim's explicit intention to suggest a
philosophy for Reform Judaism or not, there are two ways
in which he contributed importantly to it. First, his philosophy allows the possibility that a new revelation can be given
to the men of his own time. This is necessary to offset the
claim of traditionalists that the Word of God has been given
once and for all time, and it also permits the working out
of a reform based upon the newly revealed truth. In the
second place, Steinheim's contention that not every word of
the Bible is genuinely revelation allows a selective acceptance
of biblical revelation. Since he does not define the criterion
of selection, except by the existential suggestion of the act
of faith, his philosophy admits of a different selection by
every age, according to the conditions of its own life, and
thus sets up the possibility of a revision of theology.

The work of Samuel Holdheim (1806–60) had less philosophic importance than that of Steinheim.[21] In other respects, however, he was a far more significant figure in the
development of the Reform movement. As the first rabbi of

the Reform congregation in Berlin and one of the organizers of the Brunswick Rabbinical Conference of 1844, and as a contributor to collective attempts to express the spirit of German Reform Judaism, Holdheim's place in the history of the movement is secure. In the context of Reform Jewish philosophy, his particular contribution is to be found in his insistence that even divine law is given for a particular time and place. Several of his statements to this effect are very striking. One of the most notable is this:

The present requires a principle that shall enunciate clearly that a law, even though divine, is potent only so long as the conditions and circumstances of life, to meet which it was enacted, continue; when these change, however, the law also must be abrogated, even though it have God for its author. For God himself has shown indubitably that with the change of the circumstances and conditions of life for which He once gave those laws, the laws themselves cease to be operative, that they *shall* be observed no longer because they *can* be observed no longer.[22]

The particular application of this general thesis that Holdheim made in his book, *Das Ceremonialgesetz im Messiasreich* (The ceremonial law in the messianic era), published in 1845, was that the claim of the adherents of the traditionalist position that the ceremonial law is eternally valid is unfounded. It was in this book that Holdheim set forth his most often quoted words: "The Talmud speaks with the ideology of its own time, and for that time it was right. I speak from the higher ideology of my time, and for this age I am right." [23]

The greatest architect of a philosophical synthesis for German Reform Judaism was Abraham Geiger (1810–74). Geiger took from the Protestant thinkers of German romanticism, especially from Friedrich Schleiermacher, an emphasis on the inwardness of religion. Of course, the idea of inwardness was not new in Judaism; it had been one of the central themes of the Kabbala and was most important in the pietistic cult of Hassidism. The most proper description of Geiger's achievement may well be that under the stimulus of romantic philosophy he was led, from a rational standpoint, to re-affirm an older Jewish conception of piety. But the chief effect of the emphasis on inwardness is to cut the ground from under the ritualistic and ceremonial emphases of the traditionalist, rabbinic position. For if religion is, as Geiger puts it, the attitude generated by man's simultaneous con-sciousness of his "eminence and lowness, the aspiration to per-fection, coupled with the conviction that we can not reach the highest plane," [24] then theology and ritual, belief and ceremonial, are at best secondary and derivative from per-sonal attitudes and have no compelling force.

Having used this argument to mitigate the force of tradi-tionalism, Geiger made a positive and specific contribution to the discussion of the consequences for Judaism of the emancipation of the Jews. In this aspect of his thought there are clear traces of Geiger's familiarity with the Hegelian dialectic. Throughout the history of the Jews and Judaism, Geiger says, there has always been a tension between the Jewish sense of nationality, leading to such claims as that of the "Chosen People" doctrine, and the sense of universality. This tension is not peculiar to Judaism; every people goes through some such development. Every people, at some time in its history, finds its particularism generating its own an-tithesis, universalism. The uniqueness of Judaism, according to Geiger, is that, over the course of the centuries, it has worked its way through this polarity to a point where the sense of nationality has yielded completely to the sense of universality. "Judaism," he says, "has proved itself a force outliving its peculiar nationality, and therefore may lay claim to special consideration." [25] The implication of this assertion for Reform Judaism is that it can, without loss, eliminate the surviving particularistic expressions in its liturgical and doc-trinal formulations. Most significantly Reform liturgy can cut out any reference to the "Chosen People" doctrine. In Geiger's interpretation there is nothing left that can conflict with total political allegiance to any modern nation. Even before Geiger, Reform ritual had excised this doctrine from its liturgy and also had edited out all references in the traditional prayers to a return to Zion. The doctrine of a personal Messiah, so centrally important in earlier Judaism, was transformed, though with less care and consistency, into a doctrine of a Messianic Age, in order to avoid any hint of Jewish particularism. From its inception Reform Judaism involved a reforming of traditional doctrine to accord with the needs of an era of emancipation; Geiger gave this tendency its theoretical justification.[26]

## STIRRINGS ON THE AMERICAN SCENE

In the American synagogues, from the beginning, the general attitude had been one of acceptance of tradition without any clear sense of what the tradition was. One of the decisive factors in defining the attitude of the Jews of early America toward their Judaism is that there were no men of Jewish learning, no legists, no ordained rabbis, scarcely even a slightly informed layman, on the American scene. When it was absolutely necessary that an informed opinion on some matter of Jewish law be given, the lay authorities of the various synagogues in America wrote to the rabbis in Holland or in England stating the facts and requesting an interpretation. Even when these letters were answered—and there is no reason to believe that they invariably were—there was a time lag of up to a year, and it is improbable that the impatient petitioners always waited, for example, for a decision on the legality of a marriage. A second factor in defining American Jewry was that there were no pre-emancipation Jewish communities to survive into an era of emancipation. There was, in fact, no organization of the Jews except their voluntary banding together into synagogues. These synagogues had, therefore, to assume the functions that had been carried out by the European communities. If there was to

be any Jewish schooling, the synagogues had to make themselves responsible for it. If proper precautions were to be
taken with regard to the dietary laws, the synagogues had to
take these precautions. If there was to be a burial ground
for the Jews of any American city, the synagogue had to take
care of it. If philanthropic and welfare activities were to be
maintained, this, too, had to be done by the synagogues.[27]
This American tendency to synagogal autonomy was fostered
also by the general pattern of congregationalism that dominated the American Protestant scene and was even, in a number of states, made the basis of the laws governing the in-
corporation of religious groups.

Because of the absence of a communal superauthority and
of a trained body of religious leaders, it was technically and
legally possible for a group of Jews to band together at will
to form a new synagogue, even in cities where there was already an existing synagogue. The earliest examples of this
process, in Philadelphia and New York, came about because
the older synagogues, originally founded by Jews of an Iberian background and tradition, followed the Spanish and Portuguese customs (*minhag sepharad*), while the newer immigrants, chiefly from England, Holland, and Germany, were
accustomed to the German patterns (*minhag ashkenaz*). That
these early divisions could be established on the basis of differences in custom within traditionalism indicated the possibility of later establishment of synagogues on the basis of a
desire to reform the ritual. Whereas, in Berlin, when an attempt was made to set up "private" reform congregations, it
could be halted by an appeal to the Prussian government, in
America no such appeal was possible. The government had
no authority to control religious matters.

Congregation Beth Elohim of Charleston, South Carolina,
was, in the 1820s, one of the most firmly established synagogues in the United States. Charleston at this time probably had the largest Jewish population of any American city,
although New York City was challenging its lead and was
soon to become the largest center for the Jews of America.

Many of the leading Jewish families of Charleston were able to afford higher education for their children. It was among these better educated Charlestonians that the impulse to petition for a reform of the ritual of the Charleston synagogue was born. In 1824 forty-seven of them drafted a "memorial" urging changes. The petition by no means suggested a rejection of the doctrine of the "Chosen People" comparable to that of the German reformers. Indeed, the memorialists speak of themselves as "inheritors of the *true faith,* and always proud to be considered by the world as a portion of 'God's chosen people.'" Despite this, they say that they have become alienated from the synagogue, and attribute their alienation to "certain defects which are apparent in the present system of worship." [28]

Their suggestions for change were, then, altogether concerned with matters of ritual. They called for English translations of some of the most important prayers and for the institution of an English sermon. Their awareness of the educational function of the sermon in the Christian churches of their environment is evident:

What then is the course pursued in all religious societies for the purpose of disseminating the peculiar tenets of their faith among the poor and uninformed? The principles of their religion are expounded to them from the pulpit in the language that they understand; for instance, in the Catholic, the German and the French Protestant Churches: by this means the ignorant part of mankind attend their places of worship with some profit to their morals, and even improvement to their minds; they return from them with hearts turned to piety, and with feelings elevated by their sacred character.[29]

The petitioners urged that only the most important parts of the service should be retained, but that attention should be given to presenting those parts most impressively. They pointed to the improvement of attention and decorum, especially in "the younger branches of the congregation," that would follow on the "alterations" they proposed.

Included in this memorial there is a translated passage

attributed to "the *Frankfort Journal*" which indicates that
these Charlestonians were aware of the beginnings of the
Reform movement in Germany. More fundamentally, since
German reform had not at this time made any great progress,
it is clear that the Charleston memorialists regarded themselves as the vanguard of enlightenment:

From the above extract, it appears, that no climes, nor even
tyranny itself, can forever fetter or control the human mind; and
that even amidst the intolerance of Europe, our brethren have
anticipated the free citizens of America in the glorious work of
reformation. Let us then hasten to the task with harmony and
good fellowship. We wish not to *overthrow,* but to *rebuild;* we
wish not to *destroy,* but to *reform* and *revise* the evils complained
of; we wish not to *abandon* the institutions of Moses, but to
*understand and observe them;* in fine we wish to worship God,
not as *slaves of bigotry and priestcraft,* but as the enlightened
descendants of that chosen race, whose blessings have been scattered throughout the land of Abraham, Isaac and Jacob.[30]

When their fellow-members of Congregation Beth Elohim
refused to consider the changes proposed in this memorial,
twelve of the dissident group, later joined by others, resigned
and founded a new congregation, called "The Reformed Society of Israelites."

For a time the new society flourished. Its *Constitution* was
printed in pamphlet form, and was later given a laudatory
review in *The North American Review* for July, 1826. The
reviewer, Samuel Gilman, also gave flattering notice to the
first anniversary discourse, delivered by Isaac Harby.[31] The
*Constitution* includes a declaration of faith, the form of
which was based on Maimonides's Thirteen Articles; but the
number was reduced to ten and the content was changed by
the omission of the belief in the Messiah and in bodily resurrection.[32] Harby's discourse stressed the continuity of the
work of the Reformed Society of Israelites with the general
progressive development of liberal tendencies in Europe and
America as a consequence of enlightenment. Thomas Jeffer-

son commented, in a letter to Harby: "Nothing is wiser than that all our institutions should keep pace with the advance of time and be improved with the improvement of the human mind." [33] The address at the second anniversary of the society was delivered by Abraham Moise, who further developed the theme of participation in enlightenment:

We claim, then, to be the advocates of a system of rational religion; of substance, not form. For this we hold ourselves responsible to God and Our Consciences. We look not to the antiquity of rites and ceremonies as a just criterion for their observance by us, but to their propriety, their general utility, their peculiar applicability to the age and country in which we live, to the feelings, sentiments and opinions of Americans.[34]

All in all, the omens were propitious, and Gilman was not altogether out of line in his prophecy that "the spirit of the age, like the voice of Jehovah, will gently and irresistibly convert the present synagogue, with its obsolete ceremonials, its unintelligible language and its alleged unimpressive influences, into a more rational sanctuary." [35]

Gilman was wrong, however, because he failed to foresee the decline of Charleston, which went downhill rapidly after 1828. By 1833, just before its tenth birthday, the Reformed Society of Israelites was dissolved. The first experiment in American Reform Judaism had fallen victim to external circumstances beyond its control. But it was not by any means a failure, for in 1836 the parent congregation, Beth Elohim, chose as its rabbi Gustave Posznanski (1804–79), who was sympathetic to Reform. Poznanski, although Polish born, had been educated in Hamburg and was in close accord with the thinking of the members and leaders of the Hamburg Temple. Through him the Charleston reformers triumphed, for, despite much controversy, Poznanski remained as rabbi of Congregation Beth Elohim until 1860, and even after his tenure the Congregation remained in the Reform camp.[36]

CONTROVERSIES AND CONFERENCES IN GERMAN REFORM

The sporadic establishment of Reform congregations in Germany, in the face of great opposition from the traditionalist party; the controversies engendered by the publication of prayer books for use in these congregations; and most interestingly the so-called Geiger-Tiktin Affair—a controversy occasioned by the appointment of Abraham Geiger, an outstanding leader of the Reform faction, as rabbinical colleague of Solomon A. Tiktin, one of the most unyielding of the advocates of traditionalism, in Breslau in 1839—all made it clear that the Reform group had somehow to find a united voice if the single voice of traditionalism was to be countered. What was at stake was not only the future of the Reform movement in German Jewry but also the future of the ancient Jewish tradition of freedom of inquiry.

As early as 1837, while he was still rabbi of the Jewish congregation in Wiesbaden, Geiger had proposed that the progressive rabbis should hold a conference, out of which, he hoped, would emerge a platform on which the Reform movement could unite. The problem, as Geiger saw it then, was that each individual and each little reformist group was making its own judgment of what was essential and what nonessential in the Jewish tradition. This could lead only to anarchy, in which each little fragment would become a law unto itself. Two things should be noted. First, Geiger's statement did not propose that this rabbinical conference should assert itself as an ultimate authority, but only that it should be a deliberative assembly, and that its conclusions would carry weight because of the thoughtful reasoning that lay behind them. Second, the statement indicates the extent to which Geiger and those who thought as he did considered the Reform movement a spiritual revival, a deliverance from formal rigidity (*Formenstarrheit*). The actual conference held at Wiesbaden in August, 1837, was not very productive and certainly did not live up to Geiger's great hopes.[37] The results came later at conferences held at Brunswick (1844), Frankfort (1845), and Breslau (1846).

Between the pioneering Wiesbaden conference and the more successful later assemblies occurred the Geiger-Tiktin Affair, which may have contributed greatly to the success of the later conferences by polarizing the thought and sentiment of the rabbis of Germany into old and new school factions.[38] Rabbi Tiktin, who had been spiritual head of the Breslau Jewish community since 1821, held the old-fashioned conception of the rabbi as chiefly the communal authority on Jewish law. He had no sympathy with the desire of members of the community for a preaching rabbi, in tune with the newer age. He viewed as no concern of his the drifting of many Jews away from the community; he simply could not understand that a major reason for this drift was that the principles of Judaism were not being taught to the young in an understandable and comprehensible fashion. When the authorities of the community failed to convince Tiktin that he had a responsibility in this matter, they agreed to search for a colleague whose learning was recognized, but who was also able to preach in German, to interpret Judaism in terms of the modern spirit, and to supervise the education of the Jewish youth of the community, using modern educational methods. Abraham Geiger was the man chosen, and the battle lines were immediately drawn, for his advanced views were well known.

Many of the methods used by both sides in the ensuing controversy were petty and far beneath the dignity of the occasion and the question involved. Indeed, Dr. Gabriel Riesser (1806–63), who was already respected as the foremost spokesman for complete emancipation of the Jews, was moved to write:

May those who represent advanced views bear in mind that true wisdom is always joined with mildness, that malice never converts the erring but strengthens him in his attitude, and that it is very unfitting to combat error (so long as this does not assume the aspect of injustice) with the weapons of hatred. But may those others who do battle for traditional opinions recognize that personal persecution, intrigue, and calumny have as their only result the dishonoring and shaming of the cause they mean to serve.[39]

Riesser's noble words did not put an end to the use of the methods of contention that he deplored, but in the end Geiger's election was validated by the Ministry of Public Worship of Prussia. In his inaugural sermon Geiger pulled no punches; he called for the rejuvenation and renovation of Judaism to enable it to assume a higher and better position in the world. "Judaism is not a finished tale; there is much in its present form that must be changed or abolished." [40]

Rabbi Tiktin, of course, could not accept Geiger or Geiger's position. He and his supporters refused to recognize the validity of Geiger's appointment. He sought the opinions of like-minded rabbinical upholders of the Talmudic tradition, chiefly from sections of the country to which enlightened ideas had not penetrated, and published these in 1842 in a small volume called *Darstellung des Sachverhältnisses in seiner hiesigen Rabbinatsangelegenheit* (An exposition of the state of affairs in the matter of the rabbinate in this place). Tiktin's own words in this pamphlet make clear that there could be no compromise: "Whoever disregards any command or prohibition of the Talmud must be considered an unbeliever and as standing outside the pale of Judaism, and is therefore an untrustworthy witness." [41] The right of free inquiry, a right that is central to the Talmud itself, was denied by these latter-day partisans of Talmudism. All the rabbis who contributed to the Tiktin pamphlet were in agreement that not a jot or tittle of the Talmudic legislation was subject to any change whatsoever, regardless of the conditions of any particular time and place, except by established procedures of rabbinical enactment which, once made, had the force of the most ancient of legislation.

The Breslau authorities had found themselves forced to suspend Tiktin from his position because of his intransigency. Now they were impelled to seek a reply to the central question raised by Tiktin's *Exposition*. They wrote to a large number of leading rabbis in various parts of Central Europe in these terms:

The question to be decided is whether progress is possible in Judaism or whether strict fixedness is commanded; whether the great number of our coreligionists, who entertain opinions about the value and validity of Talmudical enactments different from those held in former centuries, may still claim the name Jew or are to be considered unbelievers; whether Jewish theology can endure scientific treatment and free investigation or whether the traditional views which are at variance with all culture may not be touched, nay, not even examined, and whether a man who champions openly and strives eagerly to spread a free, scientific, Jewish-theological conviction is entitled to occupy the rabbinical office or is unfitted for it.[42]

The replies they received were published in two volumes (1842 and 1843) with the title *Rabbinische Gutachten über die Verträglichkeit der freien Forschung mit dem Rabbineramte* (Rabbinic opinions concerning the compatibility of free inquiry with the rabbinical office).

These opinions would be well worth examining in detail. They were forthright and direct assertions of the right of free investigation, and often the authors supported their assertions by citations to the Talmud itself. In addition they indicated that it is not change but resistance to change that is the novelty in Jewish life. One of the older rabbis who contributed an opinion declared that "the ancient sages and interpreters did not desire to prevent later generations from modifying their decisions in accordance with the changed needs and circumstances of their age."[43] He also pointed out that Jewish teachers in every age have always followed the biblical pattern of investigating the reasons for all the regulations. Because they carried out this sort of inquiry, they were always prepared to reform "the ritual as often as they considered it necessary, and changed conditions have not diminished in the least this right to reform for modern Jews." [44] More important than the details, however, was the renewed indication that the impulse to reform was widely prevalent and historically justified, and that there was a large body of rabbis whose combination of traditional lore and modern knowledge qualified them to define the form of Jewish spirituality appropriate to enlightened men living in a modern emancipated Western European environment.

Many of the rabbis who contributed to the two volumes of *Rabbinische Gutachten* also attended and participated in the protracted discussions at the Brunswick, Frankfort, and Breslau conferences. [45] The explicit purpose of these conferences was to adapt the essentials of Judaism to the practical conditions of nineteenth-century life. To approach this purpose it was necessary to cover some basic theoretical questions, such as the right of such a conference to make proposals for reform, and the precise degree of authority retained by the Talmud. It was equally necessary, and more directly relevant, to discuss more practical and immediate issues: the intermarriage of Jews with Christians and whether a rabbi was permitted to solemnize such a union; the relation of religious and ethnic elements in Judaism, leading to the question of the political affiliation of the Jews; the reform of the liturgy, including the question of the extent to which Hebrew should continue as the chief language of Jewish prayer, and that of the permissibility of organ music in the synagogue; opposition to the special form of oath (*more Judaico*) humiliatingly administered to Jewish witnesses in courts, a barbarous relic of medievalism; the validity of special Jewish traditional laws regarding marriage and divorce; criticism of the dietary laws, of the rigidities of Sabbath observance, and of "superstitious" practices such as circumcision. [46] In addition to these questions, on which some of the participants, and even some of the organizers, felt that the conferences had been entirely too negative and critical, there was, at the Frankfort conference, an extended and heated discussion of the interpretation of the Messianic doctrine; the more radical of the reformers stood firmly for a universalistic hope of a Messianic age for all mankind while the more traditionally minded insisted upon retention of the idea of a personal Messiah who would establish a restored Jewish state. The purpose of this discussion was not to resolve the theological question, however, but rather to provide a basis for evaluating liturgical references to the Messianic idea. Despite all the opposition that these conferences engendered, both from traditionalists who felt that they had gone much too far and from ultrareformers who felt that they had not gone far enough, the three rabbinical conferences of 1844–46 demonstrated their value by confronting openly the most touchy questions in the adjustment of Judaism to modernity. Geiger was surely justified in declaring: "The rabbinical Conference is the most powerful agent for progress in Judaism, the institution which will show itself more and more capable of meeting the needs of our religious conditions." [47]

### THE PROGRESS OF REFORM JUDAISM

The decade of the 1840s is a watershed in European life. After the Napoleonic era, from the time of the Congress of Vienna (1815), Europe was in the grip of reaction, drawing back from the political and economic implications of the Enlightenment. In the 1840s the submerged liberal and radical forces regrouped themselves for a renewed attack on the ancient citadels of privilege. The widespread revolutionary movements of 1848, whether successful or unsuccessful, stand as a permanent monument to the resurgence of European liberalism. Surely in the light of the general thesis that movements in Judaism are responsive to the environments in which Jews live, we might expect to find that the Reform movement showed major progress during this critical decade.

Reform had established a foothold in Germany and a toehold in France and the United States before 1840; by 1850, in addition to strengthening its position in Germany, both by establishing new congregations and by the rabbinical conferences, the Reform movement had gained new positions in Hungary and in England and had laid down firm roots in the United States.

For the later history of the Reform movement the American developments are unquestionably of first importance. Immigration, chiefly from Germany, had more than doubled America's Jewish population during the 1830s, and the movement continued through the 1840s and 1850s. Among those who came to the United States during these years there were some whose previous education qualified them to take rabbinical positions and to assume the leadership of American Jewish Reform. Thus Dr. Leo Merzbacher became rabbi of Temple Emanuel of New York at its foundation in 1845 and continued in that post until his death in 1856.[48] Even before the foundation of Temple Emanuel, a small Reform congregation, Har Sinai, had been started in Baltimore by a group of young men whose thinking had been influenced by that of the Hamburg Temple: this group had, at first, no rabbi; the members of the congregation themselves conducted the services, using the prayer book published by the Hamburg Temple.[49] At this time, too, began the distinguished American career of Rabbi Isaac M. Wise.[50] Soon after he migrated to the United States from Bohemia Dr. Wise was named rabbi of the synagogue in Albany, New York. Immediately he introduced several practical reforms—a mixed choir, the confirmation ceremony, and the substitution of family pews for the separate men's and women's sections of the synagogue. In 1850 Dr. Wise attended a public debate between Gustave Poznanski and Morris Raphall, a spokesman for traditionalism; in the discussion that followed, Dr. Wise was put by Raphall into the position of having to state categorically whether he believed in the coming of the Messiah and in bodily resurrection. Dr. Wise answered in the negative. The orthodox reaction in his Albany congregation was so sharp that, on the Jewish New Year's Day (*rosh ha-shanah*) of 1850, Wise was removed bodily and forcibly from his pulpit. His supporters withdrew from the congregation and established a new congregation, Anshe Emeth, following their rabbi into the Reform group.

Four years later Dr. Wise left Albany to become the rabbi of the oldest synagogue in the midwest, Temple Bene Israel of Cincinnati; shortly thereafter the other synagogue in Cincinnati, Bene Yeshurun, also transferred its allegiance to the Reform movement by electing Dr. Max Lilienthal as its rabbi.[51] In 1856 the first Reform congregation in Philadelphia came into being as the successor to a "Reform-Gesellschaft" that had existed in that city for nearly ten years.[52] In 1858 Chicago entered the lists with a "Reform Verein," which became Temple Sinai in 1860.[53] By the time of the Civil War, then, there was the nucleus, in the United States, of an organized Reform movement. In addition there was the beginning of a rabbinical leadership; some of these leaders have already been mentioned. Others were David Einhorn, whose reputation as a radical reformer was made while he was still in Germany, and who became the spokesman for the most radical wing of American Reform when he was rabbi of the Baltimore Reform Temple after 1855; Samuel Adler, who succeeded Merzbacher at Temple Emanuel in New York in 1857; and Bernard Felsenthal, who led the Chicago Reform Temple.[54] Others came to the New World just after the Civil War, following the lead of Samuel Hirsch who accepted the rabbinate in the Philadelphia Temple in 1866.[55] The names of these men clearly evince the German inspiration of the American Reform movement at this time; their ideas reveal this origin even more clearly.

A typical statement from these early years, indicating the major issues as these were seen at the time, can be found in Samuel Adler's reply to the question "What course should a

reformed congregation pursue?"—a question put to him by
the Chicago group a little while before they organized Sinai
Temple. His reply indicated that

The first and most important step for such a congregation to take
is to free its service of shocking lies, to remove from it the mention of things and wishes which we would not utter if it had to be
done in an intelligible manner. Such are, the lamentation about
oppression and persecution, the petition for the restoration of
the sacrificial cult, for the return of Israel to Palestine, the hope
for a personal Messiah, and for the resurrection of the body. In
the second place, to eliminate fustian and exaggeration, and, in
the third place, to make the service clear, intelligible, instruc-
tive, and inspiring.[56]

That the congregation took this suggestion, and probably
others received after similar solicitation, seriously is indicated
by the constitution that they drafted for their Temple. After
presenting their object as "fostering the inestimable inheritance of our fathers, . . . restoring the original spirit of sim-
plicity, purity, and sublimity in Judaism, and thus to per-
petuate the same and secure its duration," the incorporators
sketched the means they proposed to use for its achievement
under three heads:

1. A divine service, which, without divesting the same of its specific Jewish character, shall be in consistence with the laws of reason and truth, and which, in its form, shall be such as will meet
the demands of our time, claiming public instruction from the
pulpit as a part of the same.
2. A sound religious education for the rising generation, by sus-
taining a school in which at least a thorough instruction in religion, Hebrew, and the branches connected therewith, be im-
parted—a school inspiring the tender hearts of the children for
Judaism, and for everything that is good, just, and noble.
3. The removal of usages and ceremonies partly outlived and
partly based upon erroneous conceptions, and the substitution of
others more vital, more truthful, and more apt to produce blissful
effects, and the formation of such arrangements and institutions
which tend directly or indirectly to promote and fulfill the

objects of religion and to advance its professors to a higher stage of perfection.[57]

American Reform Judaism in 1860 was still marked by its espousal of enlightened ideas and ideals.

In addresses and articles Reform leader after Reform leader presented the approach to Judaism in the spirit of the most optimistic voices of the nineteenth century. Lilienthal, in 1854, took up the theme of the "transient and the permanent," which Theodore Parker had raised in the Christian context a decade before.[58] Lilienthal asked, "when religious ceremonies have to yield to the necessities of life and when they have to be kept at any price, subjugating life and its exigencies . . . . what in our law is God's command and what is the transient work of mortal man." [59] Einhorn urged that "the divine law has a perishable body and an imperishable spirit. The body is intended to be the servant of the spirit, and must disappear as soon as bereft of the latter." [60] The Decalogue, he insisted, is the spirit; all the rest of the ordinances "are only *signs* of the covenant."

Not that man will ever be able to dispense altogether with visible signs, but the expression and form of these must necessarily change with different stages of culture, national customs, industrial, social, and civil conditions, in short with the general demands of the inner and outer life. As little as the ripe fruit can be forced back into the bud or the butterfly into the chrysalis, so little can the religious idea in its long process from generation to maturity be bound to one and the same form.[61]

The attempts on the part of earlier generations of Jews to hold fast to the external forms, to give to the ceremonial wrappings an immutability like that of the spiritual essence, led to the confounding of the religious form with the religious spirit, so that "instead of striving to spiritualize the form, the spirit was formalized." [62]

Bernard Felsenthal hewed to the same line: "There is but one class of laws which . . . have eternal validity, and these are the moral laws, engraved by the finger of God with ine-

radicable letters in the spiritual nature of man." [63] Even the
biblical laws, when they have lost their power to exert a hal-
lowing influence on men, have no further reason to be maintained. How much more, then, have those post-biblical laws
of the Talmud and the rabbis to be subjected to investigation, to be separated into the still worthwhile and the now
antiquated? Nevertheless, the mission of Reform is not merely
to abrogate the irrelevant, but also, and more importantly,
to nurture the valuable.

Doctrines which we have recognized as true, but which have lost
in great part their hold on our contemporaries, must be implanted anew and more firmly; institutions which have a hal-
lowing influence on the religious nature, and which are likely to
enhance the religious life, must be retained, suitably changed, or,
when necessary, created anew, according to the needs and circumstances. [64]

There was still matter for controversy with such traditionalists as Isaac Leeser, editor of *The Occident and American
Jewish Advocate,* the oldest American-Jewish periodical, and
minister of the orthodox synagogue, Mikveh Israel, in Philadelphia. Leeser was not wholly opposed to any changes in
synagogue practice. He was firmly convinced, however, that
whatever changes in law were made must have rabbinical
authorization, which could come only from a synod—and
there was no synod. Another of Leeser's arguments against
the Reform leaders was that they were German-speakers;
Leeser himself was an earlier migrant from Germany and had
learned fairly good English. There was considerable animus
in his editorial advocacy of a school for advanced Jewish
studies to train English-speaking scholars for the ministry.
As far back as 1847, in an editorial, he had urged that such
a school be established, "whether in England or America,
whence may issue men of ample religious and literary en-
dowments, known to the congregations, and therefore likely
to be chosen with a full knowledge of their personal history,
in addition to that of their acquirements." [65] Leeser certainly

intended the implication here that the "personal history" of some of the imported German-speaking rabbis was unvalidated. Leeser did not succeed in founding such a school, and others who tried to establish the sort of school that he envisaged were no more successful. Even Isaac M. Wise, with his great genius for organizing, failed in a first attempt, in 1854, to set up a "Zion Collegiate Institute."

On his second attempt, Wise did not fail. With the cooperation of his fellows in the Reform movement and some of the more traditionally minded rabbis, including Sabato Morais, Leeser's successor at Mikveh Israel, Wise founded the Hebrew Union College, in Cincinnati, dedicated to the training of young men for the rabbinical office. The College opened in 1875 with four students, the first of many who were to pass through its doors to be trained for the American rabbinate. Because his own position was moderate and because he succeeded, for a time, in keeping the spokesmen for more radical reform from having a decisive voice in the policies of the college, Wise was able, for some years, to retain the good will of elements in the American-Jewish public that would not have supported an extreme program. It is possible that he lost that support partly as the consequence of a caterer's error: at the banquet in 1883 celebrating the graduation and ordination of the first four American-trained rabbis, shrimp, a ritually improper food, was served. The incident caused, as may be imagined, quite a stir.[66]

Undoubtedly there were other, more fundamental reasons why Wise lost the support of his friends among the traditionalists at this time. Although he had tried to remain on the sidelines in the controversy between Rabbi Kaufmann Kohler (1843–1926), the greatest of American Reform theologians, and Alexander Kohut (1842–94), who occupied a moderate Reform pulpit but spoke for what was later to be called the Conservative position, Wise ultimately had to support Kohler.[67] Again, in order to provide an organizational and a financial base for the support of the Hebrew Union College, Wise had been responsible, in 1873, for the establishment of the Union of American Hebrew Congregations, which, by virtue of the dominance of the Reform groups in it, soon became the national organization of Reform Jewish congregations, rather than, as Wise had hoped, a central body representative of all shades of Jewish opinion. Furthermore, again due to Dr. Wise's prodding, a conference of rabbinical adherents to Reform was held in Philadelphia in 1869. At this meeting a statement of principles was produced denying the traditional Messianic doctrine; reinterpreting the destruction of the Second Commonwealth as a necessary prelude to the dispersal of the Jews to carry on their divine mission among the nations rather than apart from them; rejecting the hope for the reinstitution of the sacrificial cult and Aaronic priesthood; translating the "Chosen People" doctrine into universalistic terms; denying the belief in resurrection of the body; and urging, in somewhat veiled language, the recital of prayers in the vernacular. At the same meeting resolutions modifying traditional rabbinical views on marriage and divorce were also passed. Another rabbinical conference, held two years later in Cincinnati, was responsible for much of the impetus behind the foundation of the Hebrew Union College.[68]

The decisive rabbinical conference, which made a formal split in American Jewish ranks inevitable, was held at the call of Dr. Kaufmann Kohler, in Pittsburgh in November, 1885. Kohler, with his more radical views, was in control throughout this meeting; the statement of principles produced there was called, twenty years later, by one of its youngest participants, David Philipson, "the most succinct expression of the theology of the reform movement that had ever been published to the world." [69] And Rabbi Lou Silberman, looking back from the perspective of nearly seventy years at the work of his predecessors, added the important qualification that the so-called Pittsburgh Platform was not a new departure but a summing-up of the changes that had already taken place. "The platform they produced was not something new but was the crystallization of all that had gone before, of the revaluation and transformation that the three themes of Judaism—God, Torah, Israel—had already undergone." [70] There were fifteen rabbis in attendance when the meeting was called to order, and some others came later during the three-day session. The keynote speaker was Kohler, who discussed the diversity hitherto prevailing in Reform opinion and practice and the need to develop a unifying program:

Looking at the various standpoints of progressive Jews individually or as represented in congregations, people only see that we have broken away from the old landmarks, but they fail to discern a common platform. . . . To many, Reform appeared the name for deserting the old camp and standard, while others beheld in it only anarchy and arbitrariness. Indeed, most of our so-called enlightened Jews welcomed the watchword of Reform as long as it meant emancipation from the old yoke of Law, but when it demanded positive work, the upbuilding of the new in place of the torn-down structure, they exhibited laxity and indifference. . . . It is high time to rally our forces, to *consolidate,* to build.[71]

With this, Kohler presented ten propositions as a basis of discussion, and these became the nucleus of the platform adopted by the conference.

The platform contained eight sections, each of which attempted to express clearly the standpoint of Reform Judaism on one major issue.[72] (1) The sanctity and sincerity of other religions was acknowledged, at the same time as Judaism was described as presenting "the highest conception of the God-idea as taught in our holy Scriptures and developed and spiritualized by the Jewish teachers in accordance with the moral and philosophical progress of their respective ages." (2) The Bible was "the record of the consecration of the Jewish people to its mission as priest of the one God." The concept of literal inspiration was not mentioned; by implication it was abandoned and the value of the Bible was founded on its use as "the most potent instrument of religious and moral instruction." In the discussion Kohler's motion to amend this section by including the words "divine Revelation" was defeated, because of the ambiguities in the interpretation of the idea of revelation. With the quiet abandonment of the doctrine of literal inspiration, it was possible for the platform to deny any antagonism between Judaism and the scientific discoveries of the nineteenth century. Darwinism was the issue at the time the platform was composed.[73] (3) Only the moral law in the Bible was to be regarded as binding; of the other parts of the Mosaic legislation the group accepted "only such ceremonies as elevate and sanctify our lives, but reject all such as are not adapted to the views and habits of modern civilization." (4) Dietary laws and regulations concerning priestly purity and dress were explicitly rejected. (5) The traditional Messianic concept was transformed into a universal hope for "the establishment of the Kingdom of truth, justice, and peace among all men." This change was combined with the rejection of the idea of Jewish nationhood; the Jews were designated "a religious community." (6) Judaism was declared "a progressive religion, ever striving to be in accord with the postulates of reason." Interfaith cooperation with Christianity and Islam was welcomed. (7) While retaining the doctrine of the immortality of the soul, the Reform rabbis cast out the belief in bodily resurrection and the doctrine of punishment in the life after death. (8) The participants, very much in tune with their time, introduced a plank calling for social justice. "In full accordance with the spirit of Mosaic legislation . . . we deem it our duty to participate in the great task of modern times, to solve on the basis of justice and righteousness the problems presented by the contrasts and evils of the present organization of society."

With this platform Reform Judaism had come of age as a completely self-conscious movement. It had its organizational structures—more highly developed in the United States than in Western Europe. It had its training schools for the rabbinate, both in Europe and in America. It had its rank-and-file support. Now it had a platform, by which it was judged and for which it was criticized—even though no official body ever formally accepted the Pittsburgh platform. These developments made an open split between the Reform element and other groups in Jewry inevitable. When the split came Reform Judaism stood firmly on the guiding ideals of eighteenth-century enlightenment and nineteenth-century emancipation, dedicated to the cause of universal brotherhood and unlimited progress.

# 3

# Reformulating Jewish Orthodoxy:
# Samson Raphael Hirsch and His Successors

THE EAST EUROPEAN CENTER OF JEWISH LIFE

Thus far, in discussing enlightenment and its consequences in Jewish life, especially the development of Reform Judaism, I have concentrated on Western Europe and the United States of America. The vast majority of the Jews of the world, however, did not live in the liberal democracies or in the more or less benevolent autocracies of the West. The centers in which the largest numbers of Jews lived were in Eastern Europe—Poland, Russia, and Rumania—and in the Ottoman Empire. In these countries, and thus for the overwhelming majority of the Jews, emancipation did not come until after World War I, and even then the emancipation was more formal than real. There were paper constitutions after 1919 granting the Jews full equality of rights, but, for the most part, these constitutions were cynically disregarded by the very governments that had proclaimed them. As a result, the Eastern European center of Jewish life retained into the twentieth century many of the characteristics that had distinguished the Jewries of Western Europe in the middle ages and the Renaissance. To this summary statement, I must add that, at least in Poland, the identification of Jews with middle-class economic functions was all but complete, and thus peasant resentment was keen and supplemented official policies of discrimination.[1]

Because there was comparatively little change in the environment which surrounded them, because the conditions of their own lives changed so slightly between the sixteenth and the twentieth centuries, the Jews of Eastern Europe were able to preserve almost intact the institutional arrangements that had been characteristic of all Jewish life in Europe at the earlier period. The Jewish community remained a vital and functioning body, serving the needs of the people for an intermediary between the Jews and the civil governments under which they lived but in which they did not participate. Debarred, for the most part, from all secular schooling both by official regulations and by popular prejudice, Eastern European Jews continued traditional Jewish education, now often neglected by the Jews of Western Europe. The Western European problem, for example, of a Jewish group that did not know Hebrew did not exist in Eastern Europe. Thus, much of the Jewish heritage that was dead in Western Europe remained very much alive in Eastern Europe.[2]

Again, with the progress of emancipation in Western Europe, the intellectual leaders among the Jews found careers of importance opening up for them in the secular world, and their direct services to their fellow Jews and to Judaism became peripheral aspects of their lives. The intellectual leaders among the Jews of Eastern Europe, to whom no comparable opportunities were offered, exercised their powers along traditional Jewish lines. Rabbinic learning may have reached a low estate in Western Europe as abler members of the Jewish people entered the professions or achieved positions of prominence in academic life, making significant contributions to the advance of all forms of study. Nothing of this sort happened in Eastern Europe; rabbinic learning continued to flourish because it was the chief career open to Jews with talent. This fact produces another important difference, for the two types of intellectual activity have radically different goals. The goal of academic, scientific intellectual work is innovation, the discovery of the new, extending the frontiers of man's knowledge. The object of rabbinical learning is the maintenance of the old, the traditional, the time-hallowed. The most honored intellectual method under such conditions is the pyrotechnical dialectic that demonstrates the relevance of an unnoticed sentence of the tradition to a problem currently under consideration. Virtuosity in such interpretive dialectic (*pilpul*) was a sure passport to honor and prominence.

Against the intellectualism bred in the Eastern European Jewish community by this exaggerated respect for skill in the manipulation of the language of tradition, there arose in the eighteenth century a popular pietistic revolt. Indeed so popular did this revolt, known as Hassidism, become that for a time the party supporting the intellectual approach to tradition was known as the Opponents (*Mitnagedim*). Hassidism was originally an attempt to give the devout heart as high a rank as the ingenious mind. It was no less traditionalist in its orientation; its difference was one of emphasis. After a generation of pure pietism, there arose a new *rapprochement* between the intellectualistic and pietistic wings of East European traditionalism. Many of the outstanding later leaders of Hassidism were thoroughly trained in the literature of the tradition and expert in its interpretation; at the same time the spiritual intensity of the Hassidic movement penetrated into the intellectualistic approach, so that its aridity was somewhat mitigated. Thus, in the nineteenth century, Eastern Europe maintained in living form a Jewish community in which devout piety and traditional learning went hand in hand.[3]

Where the same conditions did not exist, it was impossible to retain the vitality of Jewish traditionalism. In the enlightened and partially emancipated countries of Western Europe there was a sterility and artificiality in the traditionalist camp, and it was this that the early reformers protested most vigorously. In the belatedly medieval situation of Poland such a statement as the following, from the rabbis of Lissa, may have retained relevance as a guide to life for the Jews:

All commandments and prohibitions contained in the books of Moses, and that, too, in the form that they have received by Talmudical interpretation, are of divine origin, binding for all time upon the Jews, and not one of these commandments or prohibitions, be its character what it may, can ever be abolished or modified by any human authority.[4]

For the Western European Jew, however, even if his sympathies were generally with tradition rather than innovation, a statement like this went too far, because it placed the most trivial regulation of the rabbinic tradition on a par with the most august of the biblical ordinances and because it imposed a doctrinal requirement upon Jews everywhere. When Solomon Eger, chief rabbi of Posen, declared, in the same context of the Geiger-Tiktin Affair, that "only he can be considered a conforming Jew who believes that the divine law book, the Torah, together with all the interpretations and explanations found in the Talmud, was given by God himself to Moses on Mt. Sinai," [5] he, too, was asserting that *belief,* rather than *practice,* should be the touchstone of the Jewish faith.

#### NEO-ORTHODOXY IS BORN

In 1808, in the reaction of the Jews of Germany against the sterility of traditionalism, the term "orthodoxy" was first used as an epithet directed against the traditionalist party. Properly speaking, it should never have been used more generally, for it is only when there is an accepted "doxy" that there can be either an "orthodoxy" or a "heterodoxy." As in so many other cases in history, however, what was originally an epithet was proudly accepted as a badge; the traditionalists themselves perpetuated the use of the term "ortho-dox" for their position. More recently there has been an inclination among the traditionalists to drop the term and resist its further use; terms like "Torah-true Judaism" are preferred. Even in this term, however, there is an implication of doctrinal limitation, for the "Torah" to which "Torah-true" Jews are expected to remain true is the augmented Torah of the rabbinical tradition.

In nineteenth-century Germany a substantial fraction of the Jews recognized the validity of the Reformist critique of traditionalism but did not agree with the solutions proposed by the reformers. This should not be understood as a conflict within each person between his emotional attachment to the Jewish tradition and his intellectual pull toward modern secular knowledge. There was both an emotional and an intellectual attachment to traditional lore, and both an emotional and an intellectual attraction to secular study. Among the traditionalists of Eastern Europe the pull was almost entirely in one direction, whereas in Germany and other parts of Western Europe the Jews were drawn in two directions at once. This was the religious context in which Jewish Neo-Traditionalism, often called Neo-Orthodoxy, was born.

The first major spokesman for a neo-traditional position was Samson Raphael Hirsch (1808–88), although Hirsch was deeply influenced by his teachers Isaak Bernays (1792–1849) and Jacob Ettlinger (1792–1871). Both Bernays and Ettlinger, though profoundly traditional in their approach to Judaism, were reared in an atmosphere in which Moses Mendelssohn's effort to combine adherence to the traditions of Judaism with a modern Western secular education was attracting attention. They were among the first of the German rabbis who had a knowledge of at least some aspects of academic studies to supplement their thorough grounding in traditional rabbinics. Ettlinger, in particular, had studied history, philology, and philosophy, and transmitted his knowledge in these fields to some of the pupils in the Yeshiva (academy for Jewish studies) of which he was the head.[6] In addition to these educational influences, Samson Raphael Hirsch's parents were among those who protested most vigorously the formation of the Reform Temple in Hamburg; his grandfather, at great personal sacrifice, had established the Jewish elementary school (Talmud Torah) in the same city; and one of his great-uncles was a well-regarded writer on rabbinical subjects, the author of two widely read books. When, at the age of fourteen, Samson Raphael Hirsch decided that he wished to prepare for the rabbinic office, he had family tradition on his side and, in Bernays, a masterly teacher to guide him. To complete his preparation, Hirsch studied under Ettlinger, from whom he received rabbinical ordination; then Hirsch attended, though for only a year, the University of Bonn, supplementing his secular studies at the Hamburg Grammar School.

His background, then, as he came to the rabbinate of the Principate of Oldenburg in 1830, was very similar to that of Geiger (who was a respected friend of Hirsch at the University of Bonn) and others of the reformers. Yet he placed a different interpretation on the confused spiritual attitudes that he had found among the Jewish students at the university and that he now found among the Jewish population of Oldenburg. Where Geiger thought that what was needed was a thoroughgoing overhaul of Judaism that would make it, to an external view, like Protestantism, Hirsch felt that it was necessary to save as much of Jewish tradition as possible by discovering a way of giving meaning to the old tradition in the new situation. Unlike such spokesmen for the older traditionalism as Rabbi Tiktin, Hirsch saw the inevitability of change, but he also recognized that a method of change was itself part of the Jewish tradition. Because he had some secular education, he was free from the hysterical fear of secular learning that was a stumbling block to many older men. Instead of reacting against Reform by insisting upon a rigidity in tradition that was not traditionally there, he reacted by stressing the power of gradual change that was properly available in the rabbinic tradition.

Hirsch did not deny the charge of the reformers that the vitality and meaning had gone out of the observances of traditional Judaism. Instead of discarding the observances, however, he used his considerable powers to revitalize them and to imbue them with freshened meaning. The first major fruit of his attempt to do so was *Neunzehn Briefe über Judenthum, von Ben Uziel* (English translation, *The Nineteen Letters of Ben Uziel*), one of the classics of modern Jewish literature, which appeared in 1836. This was followed, two years later, by a sequel, *Horeb: Versuche über Jissroels Pflichten in der Zerstreuung* (Horeb: Essays on Israel's Duties in the Diaspora), a book primarily addressed to thoughtful young men and women of the age. These were but the first of a series of works that ceased only with his death. Many of his essays were, of course, polemics directed against Reform; some, however were critical of the older school of unenlightened traditionalism.[7]

Hirsch's most constant criticism of the "old believers" had to do with their refusal to permit secular education. All truth, he insisted, has one divine source, and the search for truth, in both secular and religious studies, is the fulfilment of the biblical injunction, "Know the Lord in all your ways" (Prov. iii, 6).[8] With respect to the question of the legitimacy of secular studies, he met and defeated the traditionalists on their own ground by refuting their arguments out of the very rabbinic literature they considered themselves to be defending. In addition he argued historically that a combination of Jewish studies with general knowledge had always been the pattern of studies among Jews, save during the period preceding his own. He instanced, particularly, the general knowledge displayed by the Babylonian rabbis during the great era of Jewish history in that Middle Eastern land and the contributions of rabbinically trained persons to secular knowledge during the golden age of Spanish-Jewish life.

In the return of Western European Jews to the study of general subjects at the beginning of the nineteenth century, Hirsch saw a reversion to an older and better relationship between religious and general education, not a fad born out of the Enlightenment:

We maintain that an acquaintance with all those elements which lie at the root of present-day civilization and a study of all the subjects required for such an acquaintance are of the highest necessity for the Jewish youth of our day (as it was in fact in all times), and should be looked upon as a religious duty. This will be denied by no Jew who recognizes what Judaism demands. We are ourselves fortunate enough to live in a time which we can regard as the dawn of a new era of justice in human affairs, in which the members of the Jewish people also will be invited to take an active part in all humane, social and political activities among the nations. Our contact with general culture no longer bears the passive character which it had in the times of our fathers. But even if this were not so, how religiously important it would be to provide our youth with the knowledge which would enable them to form a true and just appreciation of the personal, social, political and religious conditions and relations in which they would have to live as men and Jews. How religiously important it would be to give them the knowledge for properly appraising the European culture by which they are surrounded and for absorbing with zest all that is good and noble in it! [9]

In this matter, Hirsch's view was more in tune with that of the partisans of Reform than with that of many leaders of the Orthodox group.

A second issue on which Hirsch's Neo-Orthodoxy differed from the thought of the older traditionalists developed out of his readiness to lead a traditionalist group in secession from a Jewish community that had been captured by the Reform movement. Just as, in the earlier years of the nineteenth century, it had been possible for the traditionalist group in some communities to halt the advance of Reform, temporarily at least, by imposing the sanctions of the community organization, so, once the Reform group had taken over leadership in a community, the traditionalists had great difficulty in retaining the type of religious services and activities that they believed proper. This had happened in Frankfort, where the Reform movement had developed a great deal of strength and the small remnant of traditionalists found itself almost swamped.

By this time, in 1851, Samson Raphael Hirsch had accepted a most prominent position as the Chief Rabbi of Moravia and Austrian Silesia and had become a member of the Austrian parliament. Nevertheless, when the small orthodox fragment in Frankfort asked him to become its leader, he resigned his high office in Austria and accepted the Frankfort call. He remained in Frankfort for thirty-seven years, till the end of his life, and played a part in restoring the Jewish community of the city to preeminence. Hirsch's efforts to reinvigorate traditional Judaism in Frankfort were most successful. He began, characteristically, by instituting schools rather than by building a synagogue. "There is no hurry for a synagogue; first we need a school to build up a new generation of knowledgeable and loyal Jews for whom Judaism is their life's purpose; then we shall have a synagogue. What would be the use of a magnificent house of prayer if we had no young men and women to worship in it?" [10] Soon his schools, combining the teachings of modern and traditional subjects, had weaned enough parents away from the school maintained by the Reform group in Frankfort to achieve a student body of six hundred. While at Frankfort, Hirsch also founded a monthly magazine, *Jeschurun,* which he edited for sixteen years and to which he contributed many essays. Through this magazine he carried his cause into homes all over Germany. In addition, during this same time his scholarly writings, especially his commentary on the Pentateuch, solidified his reputation among the learned. In all these ways Hirsch gained adherents to his Frankfort congregation.[11]

So strong did the Neo-Orthodox congregation become that the dominant Reform communal authorities were compelled to yield to it in a number of ways: its new synagogue was built by the community; provisions for the maintenance of dietary regulations under the supervision of orthodox rabbis were made; even the ritual bath (*mikvah*) was rebuilt to satisfy the demands of Hirsch's minority group. In spite of all these gains, Hirsch was unsatisfied. He was conscientiously convinced that orthodox Jews should not retain membership in a community which sponsored both Reform and Orthodox activities; he was particularly concerned because some part of the taxes paid to the community by the Orthodox would be used for the support of institutions in whose programs they did not believe.

For a considerable time, however, there was nothing that Hirsch could do about this conviction. The Prussian law required a Jew to remain a member of his community unless he renounced Judaism. In 1873 the similar law with regard to Christians was changed by the government; now Christians were allowed to leave a church with which they had come to disagree without renouncing Christianity. Immediately Hirsch began a campaign to gain the same right for Jews, a campaign carried through to success in 1876, when the parliament passed the Law of Secession. As soon as the passage of this law made it legally possible for the Orthodox Jews to secede from the general community and set up a separate community of their own, Hirsch recommended to the members of his congregation that they do so. To his surprise, not all of them were ready to follow his advice. Furthermore, the opposition included Moses Loeb Mainz, a fine Talmudic scholar, who had been one of the handful of Orthodox leaders who had originally issued the call to Hirsch to come to Frankfort. Loeb and those who sided with him argued that the concessions that had been made by the existing community made secession unnecessary, especially since the communal authorities had agreed that the taxes paid by the Orthodox group were not to be used for the support of institutions operated on Reform principles.[12]

Hirsch's reply was well reasoned but less temperate than much of his polemic, perhaps because the disagreement was now within his own group. He affirmed the strong position that remaining within the Frankfort community was implicitly an admission that there was a justification for the Reform movement. Thus, he claimed, anyone who remained in the community and did not follow him in seceding from it was accepting a movement that denied what he considered the basic and holy principles of Judaism. The communal concession with regard to funds collected from Orthodox members seemed to him meaningless since all the moneys of the community were the joint property of all its members, and therefore the Orthodox members shared with the Reform members all responsibility for their use.[13] Hirsch was disappointed, too, when Seligmann Baer Bamberger (1807–78), Chief Rabbi of Wuerzburg, and a long-time opponent of Reform, sided against him with those who considered secession unnecessary. This was an especially hard blow because Hirsch had had every reason to believe that Bamberger would second his efforts for secession. Bamberger's past statements had urged secession from Reform-dominated communities, and he had even written a statement in favor of secession from the Frankfort community:

An Orthodox Jew may on no account participate in the administration of a reform community's hospital. The reason for this is clear when one considers the observance of the Sabbath and the Dietary Laws. The conscientious observance of these commandments is only possible when the administration of such institutions is placed in the hands of men of recognized orthodoxy, and for obvious reasons reformers cannot be considered reliable. . . . I would state, in addition, that the members of the executive committee of a community must be as scrupulously observant as those of a rabbinical court. . . . Hence an irreligious committee must not be recognized by orthodox Jewry and no believing Jew may become a member of it.[14]

Bamberger went on to say that since the new law had granted the right to secede, anyone who failed to secede would actually be guilty of a "breach of the above mentioned religious ordinances."

In spite of this firm stand, not two months later Rabbi Bamberger announced that in the light of the concessions made by the officials of the Frankfort community and their willingness to provide guarantees for carrying out their promises, "it could no longer be deemed necessary to secede from the Reform Community."[15] Hirsch was astounded at this sudden change of heart and addressed an open letter to Bamberger chiding him for the position he had taken. Bamberger, or perhaps one of his students, replied, and the controversy ended with a sharply worded critique by Hirsch. Apart from the merits of the case, on either side, there are two comments that should be made. One is that from the best of motives Hirsch was apparently quite willing to destroy the unity of the Jewish community which had been, for so many centuries, a major factor in strengthening Judaism against external attack. The other is that on the question of the absolute necessity of secession of the Orthodox from a Reform-dominated community, Hirsch's Neo-Orthodox view was less flexible than that of so eminent a representative of the old orthodoxy as Bamberger. Unfortunately, too, in the heat of the conflict, Bamberger (or his spokesman) had replied to Hirsch's contention that one sage was not permitted to reverse the decision of another in respect to that other's own community by saying that this principle holds valid only "if the rabbinical qualifications of both parties are equal. If, however, the second authority is recognized to have outstanding qualifications, he is not bound to give consideration to a decision which in his opinion is erroneous."[16] Thus the controversy came to involve a question of personal fitness as well as purely theoretical issues. In consequence, the rift between the two Orthodox groups in German Jewry was never healed.

### HIRSCH'S THEORETICAL STANDPOINT

Important as are these conflicts with his fellow tradition-alists in demonstrating that the new Orthodoxy was not a mere carbon copy of the old, we must remember that the major focus of attack, for Hirsch, was the Reform movement. We must keep in mind, too, that it is generally more char-acteristic of a movement of innovation to base itself upon a philosophical standpoint. Tradition usually needs no such justification; it is self-sustaining. Although it took some time for the philosophic groundwork of Reform Judaism to be made explicit, once this had been done, the traditionalist reply either had to be as well-grounded or to risk being in-effective as a means of attracting the young and better edu-cated German Jews to some form of traditional orthodoxy. Hirsch's distinction among the leaders of traditionalism was that he had a philosophy. His defense of Neo-Orthodoxy was grounded on a reasoned theoretical standpoint.

In the short tractate *Aboth* (Fathers, often mistakenly, Ethics of the Fathers) of the *Mishnah,* there appears the say-ing: "An excellent thing is study of the Torah combined with worldly occupation." [17] Hirsch chose this as the motto of the schools and of the congregation when he accepted the leader-ship of the anti-Reform group in Frankfort. He did so, how-ever, with a significant twist, for he interpreted the phrase here translated "worldly occupation" (*derekh eretz*) as the civilization of the times. Thus, as applied to his educational work, the motto could be understood as affirming that it is proper to combine study of the Torah with secular education. As applied to his larger work of religious leadership, how-ever, the motto suggested that he believed that work to be the exploration of the relations between the Torah and the civilization of the age in which one lived. He saw as the task of his times the establishment of a relation between the Torah and the ideas and values of the nineteenth century. The leaders of Reform, Hirsch insisted, were doing this too, but they were going about it in the wrong way. They were trying to use the temporary and impermanent values of the nineteenth century as a standard for judging the eternal and unchanging values of the Torah. For them, it was the civilization of the age that was supreme; to that spirit, Judaism had to conform or die. Yet he felt sure that to conform to the merely temporary was to die as Judaism. The proper way, then, he urged, was to use the eternal values of the Torah as a measure to judge the validity of the ideals of the nineteenth century. He proclaimed the supremacy of the Torah to the civilization of the passing age, but insisted upon the need for acquiring the best of the knowledge that the age had to offer.

From this standpoint Hirsch wrote *The Nineteen Letters of Ben Uziel.* In the first of these letters we are given the religious doubts and questionings of a young nineteenth-century intellectual, trying to understand the place of Judaism in an emancipated society. Young Benjamin writes that it is apparent from history that Judaism leads to the misery of its adherents, that the Torah forbids them to indulge in the pleasures of life and yet does not lead to any significant cultural advances comparable to those of many other nations of the world.

Robbed of all the characteristics of nationality, we are, nevertheless, deemed a nation, and every one of us is by his very birth doomed to form an additional link in this never-ending chain of misery. The Law is chiefly at fault for this: by enjoining isolation in life, and thereby arousing suspicion and hostility; by breaking the spirit through the inculcation of humble submissiveness, thereby inviting contempt; by discouraging the pursuit of the formative arts; by dogmas which bar the way of free speculation, and by removing, through the separation in life, every incentive to exertion in science and art, which, therefore, do not flourish among us.[18]

He questions, too, whether the concern for the petty details of everyday life among the traditionalists is not a perversion of natural morality. "The broad principles of universal morality are narrowed into anxious scrupulosity about insignificant trifles." Then he points out that observance of the many rules required of the faithful Jew is "quite impossible" since they were intended for a different age. Any attempt to adhere to the laws leads to limitations, difficulties, and embarrassments. Finally, it is idle to talk of reforming the structure, because

For this very reform everything is lacking, unity, legally constituted legislative bodies, authority. All of these efforts are only the doings of individuals, the most divergent opinions prevail among the Rabbis and preachers; while some, as enlightened men of the time, tear down, others hold fast to the rotten building, and wish themselves to be buried under it.[19]

Hirsch was certainly not blind to the critical issues of Judaism in an enlightened age.

The remaining letters are devoted to a response in detail to the challenge, or "complaint," contained in the first letter. Through the words of Naphtali, the respondent to this first letter, Hirsch presents, in systematic though simplified form, a total interpretation of the theological standpoint of an enlightened traditionalism. To understand Judaism, he asserts, it is necessary to take our starting position from within Judaism, not from outside. The reason for this is that Judaism is "an historical phenomenon." Like any other such evolving system, its present character is intelligible only as an outgrowth of its own sources, or roots. These, in the case of Judaism, are to be found in the Torah, whose object is "the finding of the true law of life." Specific regulations must not be judged in the abstract, but rather in their relation to this ultimate purpose. "We must strive to discover analytically the connection of the purpose with this particular object." [20] Hirsch's view of the universe is providential:

Behold now separately each created thing, . . . each with its special purpose and each specially adapted in its form and matter for that purpose; the same Almighty wisdom formed and designated each for its special purpose. . . . Now, notice again this great throng of beings, tho separated and distinguished by peculiar construction and different purposes, yet united in one great harmonious system, each working in its own place, its own time, and according to its own measure of force, none interfering with the other, each bearing the All and borne by the All.[21]

From this providential or teleological viewpoint, as Hirsch read the Torah, he came to the conviction that the central principle and purpose is mutual service, "continual reciprocal activity. . . . None has power, or means, for itself; it receives in order to give; gives in order to receive." [22]

Man, too, is called into being in order to serve and be served. As the highest of beings in the world, made in the image of God, man receives the most service; as he receives more, so it is his obligation to give more service to the world, to his fellow men, and to God. Man's unique distinction is his self-awareness. This does not free him *from* serving; it frees him *to* serve consciously. "The law to which all powers submit unconsciously and involuntarily, to it shalt thou also subordinate thyself, but consciously and of thy own free will. . . . Therefore thou shalt be first and highest servitor in the company of servants." We have both an external and an internal criterion for judging man's moral success; externally he is judged by the correspondence between his deeds and the will of God as expressed in the Torah, and internally he is judged by the proportion between his powers and his fulfilment of God's will. One who has great powers is obligated to exercise them greatly in the service of God; one whose powers are small is obligated only to exercise them to the extent of his capacity. "Life, therefore, may be an utter failure in spite of the purest sentiments, if the deeds done be not right; or may, on the other hand, be most sublime despite infinitesimal results, if the means did not suffice for more." Man's strength or weakness, wisdom or foolishness, wealth or poverty are predestined by divine decree; man's virtue and piety are fruits of his own free will in the exercise of his God-given powers.[23]

To proclaim that the sacred duty of man is service to God is the special mission of Israel. Israel's responsibility has been to proclaim this message both through its history and through the daily life of its people, who were commanded to make the fulfilment of the will of God their only aim. In order to carry out its mission Israel must remain ethically and spiritually separate from the other peoples of the world. The people of Israel are forbidden to live as the other peoples of the world live, because Israel may not idolize wealth and pleasure while announcing the great truth that there is one God who is the creator, the lawgiver, and the father of all beings.[24] The complex of laws, precepts, and commandments in the Torah was given to Israel alone in order to enforce its isolation from the rest of mankind. Hirsch agreed with Mendelssohn that the Torah does not contain those general truths of religion that are addressed to all mankind. It assumes these and enunciates only those special laws laid down for Israel alone. The emphasis of the Torah falls upon the observance of the law in every detail rather than upon belief in any particular doctrines. For observance of the law is the essence of Judaism, within the overarching purpose of God. God's intent in these laws was to train the Jews for their mission and destiny.[25]

Hirsch, in this way, took his stand firmly with those disciples of Mendelssohn who denied that Judaism is a creedal faith. Most emphatically he asserted that "Judaism enjoins six hundred and thirteen duties, but knows no dogmas." In the same context, he rebuked the barren intellectualism of those Jews of his time who dedicated themselves to "abstract and abstruse speculation," and he urged that the purpose of all thought is to discover our "life-duties."

True speculation does not consist, as many would-be thinkers suppose, in closing the eye and the ear to the world round about us and in constructing out of our own inner Ego a world to suit ourselves; true speculation takes nature, man, and history as facts, as the true basis of knowledge, and seeks in them instruction and wisdom; to these Judaism adds the Torah, as genuine a reality as heaven or earth. But it regards no speculation which does not lead to active, productive life as its ultimate goal; it points out the limits of our understanding and warns us against baseless reasoning, transcending the legitimate bounds of our intellectual capacity, however brilliantly put together and glitteringly logical it may appear to be.[26]

In this reproof of intellectualism, Hirsch probably had in mind the advocates of the "scientific study of Judaism" (*Wissenschaft des Judenthums*), though in this context he does not mention them by name. In a later essay, however, he speaks of the proponents of scientific method in the study of Judaism as looking down "with disdain on the cultural efforts of our past as belonging to an age of darkness and ignorance." Then he contrasts the actual achievements of the scientific study of Judaism most unfavorably with the achievements of the generations of patient study of the Torah. In the traditional method of study, life and learning were in constant relation with each other. "Life was ready for learning because learning was meant for life, because Jewish learning was quite literally the science of living. Jewish science was the theory which was to be applied to life practically." [27]

The special way of living, the special relation between life and the Torah to which Hirsch called his people, involved a spiritual isolation. Spiritual separation, however, does not necessarily imply physical segregation. He argued, indeed, that the better a Jew fulfilled his obligations as a Jew, the more respect and love his non-Jewish neighbors would have for him and the more possible would be "as great a degree of social intimacy as your life can concede." From this perspective Hirsch examined the central question of emancipated status: "the reconcilability of Gentile citizenship with the eternal ideals of our faith." He argued that it is the duty of Jews to join their fellow citizens in everything bearing upon the welfare of the community at large, because the independent nationhood of Israel was never an essential part of the mission of the people. "Land and soil were never Israel's bond of union, but only the common task of the Torah." Israel's unity is a spiritual one, not involving political life or territorial cohesiveness. There is nothing in Judaism that should lead the Jew to forego the advantages accruing to him from emancipation. Judaism is not a renunciation of life but an acceptance of service to life. "Just as it is our duty to endeavor to obtain those material possessions which are the fundamental condition of life, so also is it the duty of every one to take advantage of every alleviation and improvement of his condition open to him in a righteous way." To the extent that emancipated status would mean an increased opportunity for the Jew to fulfil his mission of exemplifying to the world a life lived in awareness of God's will, it is completely desirable.[28]

Hirsch considered the reform advocated by supporters of the Reform movement to be artificial. He said their way was to take "a standpoint outside of Judaism, to accept a conception derived from strangers, of the purposes of human life, and the object of liberty, and then, in correspondence with this borrowed notion, to cut, curtail, and obliterate the tenets and ordinances of Judaism." [29] True reform would be to reform ourselves in accordance with the eternal principles of Judaism. The Reform party seeks to ally religion to progress; Neo-Orthodoxy seeks to ally progress to religion. "For them, religion is valid only to the extent that it does not interfere with progress; for us, progress is valid only to the extent that it does not interfere with religion." [30] Basic to the Reform misunderstanding of Judaism is the analogy with the Christian church; this it is that leads the sponsors

of reform to a cavalier attitude toward the traditional "ceremonial law." But the ceremonial law is no more expendable
than is the moral law; it is part of the discipline of the Jew
for his mission.

Judaism is not a religion, the synagogue is not a church, and the
Rabbi is not a priest. Judaism is not a mere adjunct to life: it
comprises all of life. To be a Jew is not a mere part, it is the sum
total of our task in life. To be a Jew in synagogue and the
kitchen, in the field and the warehouse, in the office and the pulpit, as father and mother, as servant and as master, as man and
as citizen, with one's feelings and one's thoughts, in word and in
deed, in enjoyment and privation, with the needle and the grav-
ing-tool, with the pen and the chisel—that is what it means to be
a Jew. An entire life supported by the Divine idea and lived and
brought to fulfilment according to the Divine will.[31]

## OTHER NEO-ORTHODOX ACHIEVEMENTS

The essential contribution of Samson Raphael Hirsch to
the development of Neo-Orthodox Judaism was to propose
a justification for traditionalism that was not inconsistent
with the intellectual and practical demands of the nineteenth
century. "Enlightenment"—that is to say, modern secular
knowledge—was, for Hirsch, not inconsistent with maintenance of the Jewish tradition. In practical terms the schools
he established in Frankfort were the instruments by means
of which he demonstrated the validity of his theory. But the
instruction of rabbis still was carried on in the schools of
the Old Orthodoxy (*yeshiboth*), for the most part by teachers
who resented and resisted the incursions of studies in the
modern disciplines. Until Neo-Orthodoxy had the capacity
to train and develop its own leadership, imbued by the new
ideal, it could not become a significant movement in Jewish
life.

The creation of a modern rabbinical seminary was the
achievement of Israel Hildesheimer (1820–99). Hildesheimer

was inspired by the same teachers who had moved Hirsch, Isaak Bernays of Hamburg, and Jacob Ettlinger of Altona. It was Ettlinger, a remarkably learned man, who introduced Hildesheimer to the elements of history, philosophy, and philology. After his studies with Ettlinger at Altona, Hildesheimer went to Berlin, where he studied at the university while continuing his rabbinic studies. Later Hildesheimer attended the University of Halle and earned his doctorate in Semitic philology, writing a thesis on "The Correct Way of Interpreting the Bible." After a period spent as teacher and student in Halberstadt, where he came into conflict, after 1847, with the Reform movement, Hildesheimer was called to be rabbi in the community of Eisenstadt, in Hungary. He was the first German-trained rabbi with a modern education to be appointed to a rabbinical post in that country, where Orthodox opposition to German enlightenment was extremely strong and feelings ran high. Yet one of the conditions that Hildesheimer had made on his accepting the call to Eisenstadt in 1851 was that he would be allowed to start a modern rabbinical seminary. At this seminary, which he directed for eighteen years, students were expected to study Latin, Greek, German, and mathematics in addition to the traditional rabbinical studies which occupied so many hours.

In 1868 open discord between Orthodox and Reform elements, on the one hand, and between the *Hassidim* and *Mitnagedim* among the Orthodox, on the other, produced a rapidly degenerating situation in Hungarian Jewry. Unwilling to subject himself to the strain of carrying on his educational work under such conditions, Hildesheimer accepted a call from the Orthodox fragment of the Berlin community in 1869. He was not going into an easy situation. The dominant rabbinical figure in the Berlin community was Abraham Geiger; under his influence the community was strengthened in its adherence to the Reform standard. Hildesheimer had to wage an uphill fight to reinvigorate the last remaining elements of Orthodox Judaism. His situation in Berlin was a direct parallel to that faced by Samson Raphael Hirsch in Frankfort, and his first step in the regeneration of Orthodoxy was, like Hirsch's, to establish an elementary religious school. Later, in 1873, with considerable assistance, especially in financing his program, Hildesheimer opened a modern rabbinical seminary in Berlin. At last the Neo-Orthodox movement in Germany could express its ideal of combining modern and traditional training for its own rabbis. Needless to say, the new seminary was criticized both by the Reformers and by adherents of the Old Orthodoxy. Nevertheless Hildesheimer persisted and developed an outstanding faculty, including David Hoffmann, who later became Hildesheimer's successor as head of the school.[32]

Hoffmann (1843–1921) had been a student of Hildesheimer's seminary at Eisenstadt and had followed his mentor to Berlin. In addition he had studied at the University of Vienna for three years and also at the University of Berlin, finally receiving his doctorate from the University of Tübingen. It is his distinction to have been the first advocate of the application of scientific critical methods to the study of the major sources of the rabbinic tradition. He was also one of the earliest Jewish scholars to confront, frankly and directly, the Graf-Wellhausen school of biblical interpretation and the reading of Jewish history that flows from this interpretation. His contention was that these non-Jewish Bible critics inevitably fell into error because they did not avail themselves of the resources preserved in the rabbinic literature. By utilizing this body of material, Hoffmann thought himself able to develop a mode of biblical interpretation and criticism that was, at one and the same time, scientific and traditional. Since at this time the Graf-Wellhausen thesis was sweeping all before it, Hoffmann's resistance was evidence of an independent spirit as well as a vigorous mind. The same qualities were demonstrated in his studies of the rabbinic tradition, where his criticism is directed against those who failed to see that there was an evolution within the rabbinic literature, that the history of the texts could be rediscovered by careful analysis. It is particularly interesting to note that Samson Raphael Hirsch approved thoroughly of David Hoffmann's critical and scientific studies of the Bible, since these studies tried to counter the effects of Protestant Bible criticism, but disapproved when Hoffmann applied the same methods to the study of the rabbinic literature.[33]

The work of the leaders of Neo-Orthodox Judaism who have been discussed here, as well as that of colleagues of comparable views but lesser achievements, was important in holding off the drift of younger Jews with modern education out of the faith of their fathers. The lives and the writings of such men as Hirsch, Hildesheimer, and Hoffmann made evident to many young people that the abandonment of tradition was not a necessary consequence of modern education. The principle upon which they operated may be summed up in the words of Baruch Stern, a later head of the school started by Hirsch at Frankfort: "The integration of ancient Jewish culture with modern surroundings, to the avoidance of assimilation and the preservation of the primacy of the Torah." [34]

ORTHODOX JUDAISM IN THE UNITED STATES

It might be said with justice that in the colonial and early national periods of American history all Jews in the United States adhered to traditional Judaism. There were, as we have seen, some reservations that came to bud in the 1820s and 1830s, and a flowering of the Reform movement from the late 1840s. During the same period there was an impulse within the Orthodox group that is, in some ways, comparable to the development of Neo-Orthodoxy in Germany, but that lacked a solid theoretical formulation. Isaac Leeser, minister of the Philadelphia congregation Mikveh Israel, was the dominant figure in this early counter-Reform movement. Leeser had more education, both Jewish and secular, than any other Jewish "minister" of his times in America, but he had nothing approaching rabbinical ordination and nothing resembling a university degree. To the extent that he developed at all as a scholar, he was self-taught.[35]

Leeser became minister of the Philadelphia congregation in 1829. The following year he established a regular pattern of preaching in English at the Sabbath services. His sermons, two dull volumes of which were published, were completely traditional in their orientation, yet they reveal Leeser's belief that there should be a conscious and selective acceptance of American cultural elements into Jewish life, lest the unconscious, unthinking, and unselective espousal of Americanism should go too far.[36] In the 1830s, with great help from Miss Rebecca Gratz, Leeser tried to establish schools in which both Jewish tradition and secular subjects would be taught. He met with double difficulty. The members of his congregation were reluctant to finance his efforts adequately, and even when, in spite of this, the schools were founded, they did not send their own children to study under Leeser, so that a high proportion of his students were charity cases. In spite of these handicaps, he produced study materials, for the most part adaptations of textbooks used in England or in Germany.[37] Still following the same general pattern being followed by his better-trained compeers in Germany, Leeser began to agitate in 1847 for the establishment of a school for advanced Jewish studies; after twenty years, in 1867, with a group of coworkers, he founded Maimonides College in Philadelphia. This venture closed in 1873 for lack of support.[38]

Another way in which Leeser tried to restore vitality to the Jews of America was by his espousal of the cause of a national union or federation. In 1843 he began to edit the first significant American-Jewish periodical, *The Occident and American Jewish Advocate*. From the beginning he saw this journal both as a vehicle for presenting his traditional views to a wider public and as a means of instilling in the Jews of the country a sense of their community of interests. It was only shortly before this, in 1840, that for the first time the Jews of America had gained a sense of unity through their activities in the Damascus Affair. In the first issue of 1844 Leeser's editorial was entitled "The Demands of the Times." Here he called for a unity of religious observance under a universally accepted religious law. A month later Leeser demanded "a federative union" of all the Jews of the country. The greatest support for Leeser's proposal came from Isaac M. Wise who, while no friend to traditionalism, felt as keenly as Leeser the need for a federation of American synagogues.[39]

Wise indicated that the unity he sought should follow the lines of a moderate reform. In May, 1849, editorializing under the title "Shall We Meet?", Leeser once more endorsed the idea of a meeting of all American-Jewish congregations, but specifically rejected the view that one objective of the meeting should be a general reform of religious practices:

We should regard a general reform by the authority of a convention as the greatest evil which could by possibility befall our people. In using the word reform, we employ it in the sense which it usually bears in the present age,—*a violent change and a substitution of new notions in the place of well-established customs and opinions.* . . . But there is another reform, which looks to the removal of municipal abuses, as we may term them; . . . we see no reason why German and Portuguese Jews could not unite in one common effort to establish a better state of things, without yielding in the least their peculiarities, or their independence.[40]

Wise and Leeser were able temporarily to subordinate their different views of what had to be done in their common eagerness to develop an institutional voice for all American Jews. However, if a meeting had taken place there is no doubt that the differences between them would have come to the surface and prevented constructive action.

For all of Leeser's admission that some changes were necessary in order to hold the loyalty of American Jews to their ancestral religion, he saw a most serious difficulty: by longstanding tradition only ordained rabbis could authorize major changes in Jewish law and practice. An English sermon might be introduced without convening a rabbinical assembly and a local congregation might promulgate rules to ensure more decorous behavior during services, but changes of this sort, he recognized, were superficial and did not go to the heart of the crisis. Like Isaac M. Wise, he wanted "improvements," but he expressed a firm "desire that nothing should be done hastily, or contrary to law." His reasons for wanting improvements were like those of the reformers, "to bring the backsliders and the lukewarm back to the pale of religion." [41] He praised the leaders of English Jewry for cutting the length of the services, but insisted that beyond this only ordained rabbis could legitimately reinterpret Jewish law. Max Lilienthal, one of the leading Reform rabbis, who held proper ordination, taunted Leeser by writing, "We suppose that it is the most sincere wish of the editor of *The Occident,* that all should remain in *statu quo;* that a synod should be convened to declare innovation unlawful, and to sanction the *status quo* by their vote." [42] Leeser replied, out of his awareness that most of the ordained rabbis in the United States were of the Reform persuasion, that even rabbis cannot authorize changes made in Jewish law "not by the decrees of the Most High, but by the silent action of the age." [43] Proper reform, he said, would be to return to the just standards of the Israel of old; this was the only reform that anyone could prove to be authorized by law. Samuel Isaacs, editor of the *Jewish Messenger,* supported Leeser's position when he wrote, "We want REFORM, not in the service, but within ourselves," [44] a comment that seems to echo Hirsch's *Nineteen Letters.*

If the character of immigration to the United States had not radically changed after the Civil War, it is possible that the impulse generated by Isaac Leeser would have led to the development of a genuinely American version of Neo-Orthodoxy. In the 1870s and 1880s, however, there began a massive migration of Jews from Eastern Europe that continued until World War I and brought to American shores a Jewish population that dwarfed the older and slowly growing Western European group. The new arrivals brought with them a type of Orthodox Jewish piety that previous Jewish settlers in America had never known, not even in their Western European homelands before migration. The newcomers brought with them their own communal traditions, their own men of learning—in some few cases, men of broad learning. They brought their own semi-sacred language, Yiddish, not merely as an ancestral tradition, to be preserved out of reverence, but as a touchstone of Jewishness. The prevalence of Yiddish served, temporarily, as a barrier to Americanization, although it became, later, one of the most potent forces for Americanization. The use of Yiddish in daily communication, the publication of newspapers and magazines in Yiddish, the carrying on of instruction in the schools and preaching in the synagogues in Yiddish insulated this group of immigrants from the currents of American life for a far longer period than had been true of any previous group of Jewish arrivals. For them, America was Exile (*Galut*) in a double sense: the traditional Exile from the land of Israel, and also Exile from the only place in the world outside of Israel where a truly Jewish life could be lived.

For a time it was hoped that this group of new arrivals, adherents of the Old Orthodoxy, could form a viable alliance with Orthodox Jews of the Leeser type on the basis of their common opposition to the Reform movement. Under such joint auspices the Jewish Theological Seminary of America was founded by Leeser's successor, Sabato Morais, and others, soon after the enunciation of the 1885 Pittsburgh Platform had given decisive direction to Reform thinking.[45] For about ten years the uneasy alliance persisted; during this period there can hardly be said to have been an Orthodox movement, since its positive character was almost entirely sacrificed to the negative objective of counteracting Reform. But in 1896 the Eastern European Orthodox group founded the Rabbi Isaac Elchanan Theological Seminary, named in honor of the then recently deceased Isaac Elchanan Spektor (1817–96) of Kovno, Lithuania, one of the greatest of the nineteenth-century Eastern European Talmudists. This Yeshiva did not (in the Western sense) *educate* its students; it was strictly a training school in Talmud and rabbinic literature. When it was in operation the Old Orthodox group was in a position to deny the validity of ordination given by the Jewish Theological Seminary of America. This, of course, meant the end of the opportunistic *entente* between the two groups of adherents of Orthodoxy.

In its original intention and its original form the Rabbi Isaac Elchanan Theological Seminary was an Eastern European Yeshiva on American soil. In 1915 it was merged with another similar school, Yeshiva Etz Chaim; in 1928 it was renamed Yeshiva College; still later it became Yeshiva University. After 1915, under the presidency of Rabbi Bernard Revel, without any departure from its Orthodox pattern, the Yeshiva expanded its program of studies and was gradually transformed into a competently administered general educational institution. Since the essence of the Neo-Orthodox position is the combination of traditional rabbinic lore with modern secular studies, it is fair to say that since 1915 there has been a major Jewish seminary training Neo-Orthodox rabbis, and providing Neo-Orthodox teachers for Jewish schools and Neo-Orthodox workers for Jewish communal organizations. As the Yeshiva has moved toward a modern Orthodox position, there have been splinter groups who proclaimed themselves the true remnant of Israel and regarded the program of the Yeshiva as an unacceptable concession to America and modern knowledge.[46]

Meanwhile, Neo-Orthodoxy in America still lacks a formulation of its program; perhaps this is attributable to the fact that its modes of adjustment are themselves part of the tradition and therefore do not require statement or defense. This fact does not mean that Orthodox Judaism is unchanging, but that all changes are to be made by traditional methods of interpretation, particularly by the responses of rabbis to specific modern questions. Rabbi Leo Jung, one of the outstanding spokesmen of American Neo-Orthodoxy, considers the process of interpretation as a perennial revitalizing of Jewish law:

Even among Jews we find some who consider orthodox Judaism as out of touch with modern times. Never did they err more profoundly. Jewish law develops through application of precedent to new conditions, exactly as English or American law does. The Responsa of the rabbis, dealing with modern questions. . . . keep the Jew in rapport with changes in his environment, and with the problems of today and tomorrow. These Responsa accompany Jewish life all through history, and help the Jew to live with the Torah as with a law which is ever alive, fresh and clear with every new question and answer.[47]

In practice, however, this method makes for neither a rapid nor an adequate adjustment to the needs of local and temporary situations. One of Rabbi Jung's own illustrations makes this lag evident. "Thus, for instance, modern means of transportation, which could not have been considered in the Mishnah, are dealt with in the Responsa upon the same principles which governed the primitive traffic of Roman days and the affairs of a caravan in the time of Palestinian independence." [48]

Many Jews who are, in the best sense, "Torah-true" cannot find satisfaction in a process of adjustment that does not take account of the differences between an ancient camel caravan and a modern space capsule. Yet they are unwilling to follow the radical path of Reform Judaism in rejecting the bulk of the rabbinic tradition. To this centrist group, which calls itself Conservative Judaism, we now turn.

# 4

*The Complex Phenomenon of*
*Conservative Judaism*

THE SEARCH FOR THE MIDDLE WAY

The Jews of Western Europe, especially of Germany, faced the nineteenth-century crisis of adjustment with self-conscious awareness of both the intellectual and the political factors that were involved in it. Enlightenment and emancipation were warmly welcomed by some of them as guides in the freeing of Judaism from the accretions of centuries of life in the ghettos. Enlightenment supplied the concomitant to emancipation; it was the inner emancipation that paralleled the outward, political emancipation. Those who welcomed both forms of emancipation advocated, in different degrees, reforms of synagogue practice and of ceremonial law. They demanded that the traditions of Judaism validate themselves to university-trained, reasonable minds. The movement, in both Europe and America, that emerged from their thought emphasized the ethical contributions of Judaism, its universal aspects, its adaptability to modern conditions.

Other Jews in Western Europe, and the vast majority of

the Jews of Eastern Europe, wanted no change at all or change kept to a minimum. Some of the Eastern Europeans went so far as to oppose the emancipation of the Jews on the ground that it would make the maintenance of the Jewish tradition in its full integrity far more difficult. Others were reluctantly ready to accept a place on the nineteenth-century stage, but wanted to limit that place voluntarily in order to preserve Jewish institutions. These constituted the party I have called Orthodox. Still others saw no conflict between modern knowledge and ancient tradition, provided only that ancient tradition remained the dominant force and the criterion for judging the value of the new sciences. They were not averse to making some slight modifications in the synagogue rituals, but resisted major changes in the ceremonial law. These were the Neo-Orthodox.

Between even the most moderate of the advocates of Reform and even the most liberal of the adherents of Neo-Orthodoxy there was a wide gap. Perhaps Abraham Geiger was right when he characterized those who fell between Reform and Neo-Orthodoxy as "those who strive to combine existing concepts with the demands of deep thinking. But all too often the nostalgia of their religious ideas is influenced by forms and views which a pleasant pietism would like to maintain as its precious heritage from days of childhood." [1] Perhaps Ludwig Philippson (1811–89), a moderate reformer, was right when he described the middle group as "reformers in part; they want to cleanse the old and revitalize it spiritually." [2] Possibly, too, Samuel Cahen (1796–1862), the learned editor of *Archives Israélites de France,* an influential monthly magazine, was also correctly defining some members of the center when, in reply to the question what reforms he supported, he answered "reforms of our ritual wherever it stands in contrast to our actual habits. We support reforms which our sages would have instituted were they living in 1840. Such reforms must be agreed to by a majority of the rabbis and theologians, and must have due consideration for the minority which will have the right to reject such reforms for its own adherents." [3] Because the center was so wide, its occupants can be described in divergent ways. Some were willing to take only one step more than the Neo-Orthodox; others were unwilling to take the last step into Reform.

In the 1840s an attempt to define the centrist position was made by Zechariah Frankel (1801–75), chief rabbi of Dresden, distinguished scholar of the historical development of the legal tradition in Judaism, and later, on its establishment in 1854, head of the Rabbinical Seminary in Breslau. Frankel first tried to formulate his position in his *Zeitschrift für die religiösen Interessen des Judenthums* (Journal for the religious interests of Judaism), in 1844–45. He later came into sharp conflict with the Reform leaders over the acts of the rabbinical conferences of Brunswick and Frankfort. In 1851 Frankel founded a new and successful periodical, *Monatsschrift für Geschichte und Wissenschaft des Judenthums* (The monthly magazine for the history and scientific study of Judaism). Thus, in addition to producing scholarly publications with limited appeal, Frankel exercised a broad influence on the thinking of many Jews of his generation.

His own education included both extensive training in the rabbinical tradition and secular studies in his native city of Prague and at the University of Pesth, from which he received his doctorate in 1831. His early rabbinical career seemed to incline toward the Reform element. He was, for example, the first Bohemian rabbi to introduce preaching in German into the practice of his synagogue. In an early issue of his *Zeitschrift für die religiösen Interessen des Judenthums* he called his position "moderate reform." In the prospectus prepared to encourage subscriptions to the *Zeitschrift,* he had clearly indicated his divergence from the Orthodox party, the party of no change, when he said "We must understand that there is nothing but disaster in that kind of absence of motion and deed behind which one looks in vain for certainties." At the same time he expressed his dissatisfaction with the negativity of the Reform position. He realized that the Jewish religion faced a crisis, but believed that Jewish tradition contained within itself the materials for rising superior to that crisis.

In these pages we shall emphasize the progress of Judaism. We shall conceive it to be our task to avoid the kind of negative reform which leads to complete dissolution, but instead, to show how the teachings of Judaism itself contain the possibility of progress. . . . Many people display nothing but a dull indifference instead of the deep religiosity of former days, and we notice that there are many who, misunderstanding the depths of Judaism, wish to dissolve it in the general mood of the modern age. The synagogue faces a crisis, but this must not dishearten us nor must we give way to doubts that it can be victorious, for the innermost content of Judaism is guaranteed both in its continued existence as well as in its latent possibilities of self-development. How such development shall take place must be determined by scientific research based on positive historical foundations.[4]

With this last phrase, we come to one of the greatest difficulties in Frankel's position; he was never able completely to clarify to his own age or to ours what he meant by "positive-historical." Yet this phrase became, as Louis Ginzberg noted, "the shibboleth of the party founded by him." [5] It is helpful to recall that the term "positive," at this time, was used (e.g., by Auguste Comte) as the equivalent of "scientific."

Frankel's "positive-historical Judaism," then, represents the particular combination of traditional spirit and modern knowledge that he considered adequate to meet the needs of the new age yet firmly attached to the past. Though more radical reforms may be demanded by some Jews, he pointed out in an article in the first issue of the *Zeitschrift,* the fact that a demand for change exists does not necessarily prove that the demand is justified. "But," he went on,

on the other hand, we cannot overlook the fact that the long-standing immobility of the past needs rectification. Until a few decades ago, Judaism had for a long period been in a state of total immobility. It satisfied the people and, therefore, their teachers did not have the right to introduce reforms even if they had been able to transcend their age. The great gap between yesterday and today has still not been bridged, and the will of our people is still firmly rooted in the past. . . . Representation of the total popular will and of science—these are the two main conditions for a reform of Judaism. Next to faith, the Jew puts his confidence in science. His whole past history of study and mental orientation guarantees that, without a genuine science of Judaism, our theologians will never have any influence upon the people.[6]

Moderate reform, or "positive-historical Judaism," aims at the combination of the "two main conditions," representation of the popular will and a foundation in scientific history.

The "scientific study of Judaism" to which Frankel contributed was certainly not completely unrelated to the type of study carried on by Leopold Zunz, I. M. Jost, and the other members of the *Wissenschaft des Judenthums* group; he might be listed, with Nachman Krochmal, Solomon Judah Rapoport, Joseph Samuel Reggio, and Samuel David Luzzatto, as constituting a traditionalist wing of *Wissenschaft des Judenthums*. The difference is that Frankel made an attempt to understand the inner dynamic of the historical processes that he investigated. His studies of the history of Jewish law tried to discover what needs of the spirit of the Jewish people were given overt form through the law. Behind this effort to understand lay the conviction that Judaism is the religious expression of the spirit of the Jewish people—its "total popular will." If this be granted, then the question of the divine and supernatural sanction of a particular tradition need never be raised. As long as the tradition serves as a meaningful vehicle for the expression of the spirit of the Jewish people, it should be maintained. Meantime, full freedom should be allowed for scholarly and scientific investigations of religious as well as other subjects. Frankel or a follower of his school had, so to speak, to live with a separation of his belief and his practice. Quite conceivably his studies might lead him to conclusions that would seem to negate the authenticity of some practice; yet if that practice still expressed a spiritual concern of the Jewish people, his obligation would be to retain it. Dr. Louis Ginzberg presents Frankel's view very clearly and distinguishes between "the task of the historian," which is "to examine into the beginnings and developments of the numerous customs and observances of the Jews," and what he calls "practical Judaism," which "is not concerned with origins, but regards the institutions as they have come to be."

A particular illustration of the way in which this principle caused controversy may be of interest. From early postbiblical times, certain laws had been referred to in the rabbinical literature as "a tradition of Moses from Sinai," even though there was no biblical enactment on which they rested. This type of reference gave expression to the belief that when the written Torah was handed down to Moses at Mount Sinai he was also given the entire body of "oral law" which he then taught to Joshua, inaugurating a process of transmission by word of mouth that was ended only centuries later, when the "oral law" was finally committed to writing. This belief was used to justify the assumption of divine authority for all later law, and thus constituted the central legal fiction of the entire rabbinic system. Frankel, out of his critical scholarship, asserted that the expression "a tradition of Moses from Sinai" means only an ordinance of unknown origin and remote antiquity, the reason for which has been lost. Immediately the traditionalists, and even such a Neo-Orthodox scholar as Samson Raphael Hirsch, were up in arms, for they saw Frankel's comment as a forthright attack on the foundation of Orthodoxy. They failed to understand how Frankel separated the religious question of whether this particular tradition still expressed a living reality in the Jewish soul from the scholarly question of its origin.[7]

From this "positive-historical" standpoint, Frankel criticized the Reform rabbinical conference at Brunswick, which, to the disappointment of its sponsors and organizers, he did not attend. The article he wrote was, in its turn, subjected to very searching and scathing criticism by Reform leaders.[8] He did, however, after much persuasion, attend the second rabbinical conference, at Frankfort in 1845. After sitting quietly through quite extreme discussions concerning Sabbath regulations and marriage laws, Frankel was led to take part in the debate—and, ultimately, to walk out of the conference—over the question of the retention of Hebrew in the synagogue services.[9]

In the debate he used the term "positive-historical Judaism." His explanation of his position, though it survives only in summary form, is evidently one that would satisfy neither extreme party. Over against the Orthodox stance, Frankel insisted, "We cannot return to the letter of Scripture. There is too great a gap between it and us." But his continuation was no encouragement to the Reformers:

On the other hand, a new exegesis is subject to the changing phases of science and, therefore, also unsuitable for the construction of a firm edifice. Or shall we grant the spirit of the time its influence? But the spirit of the time changes with the time. Besides, it is cold. It may appear rational, but it will not satisfy the soul; it will not comfort, calm, or enrapture it.[10]

Undoubtedly Frankel regarded his program as one that could restore the lost unity of the Jewish people. He thought of himself as a reconciler and mediator. Yet contrary to his own best intentions he brought a new party into existence, a party that ultimately became, in the United States, the complex phenomenon called the Conservative movement.

THE HISTORICAL SCHOOL IN AMERICA

Among the American rabbis there were some who sought a middle way comparable with that which Frankel strove to present to his German colleagues. Some of these men fell closer to the Reform end of the spectrum, close enough to be called moderate reformers. Others inclined to Orthodoxy, but an Orthodoxy more modern than that advocated by the extreme supporters of traditionalism. Indeed, the more the Eastern European influence came to predominance in Orthodox circles, the harder it became for Western European trained rabbis to identify with Orthodoxy, so that these leaders found themselves gravitating toward the center. Even Isaac Leeser, who represents so well an original American impulse toward Neo-Orthodoxy, was more closely associated, near the end of his life, with the centrist group, the Historical School. Since the range of ideas in those who made up the Historical School was from Modern Orthodoxy to Moderate Reform, its principles can be characterized only in the most general terms.

The members of the Historical School recognized the permanent value of the literary and cultural monuments of the Jewish spirit, but saw these as cultural artifacts, developed in the historical growth of the Jewish people under the differing circumstances of the varying times and places in which the Jews had lived. Unlike the Reformers, they were unwilling to cut away the bulk of this slowly evolved tradition in one radical excision. Unlike the Orthodox, they did not regard every jot and tittle of the tradition as of equal (and divine) authority. Their position was, rather, that the tradition contained the responses of the Jewish spirit to the conditions of Jewish life in other times and places, and that any novelty of response in their own age had to be in consonance with the spirit revealed in the tradition as well as with contemporary needs. They were not opposed to change as such, but they insisted that the guiding principles of change had to be discovered within the experience of the Jewish people rather than outside it. Developed as it was at a time when in science, in history, and in philosophy the evolutionary motif was being explored, the Historical School in Judaism seems peculiarly an expression of a Darwinian age.

Precisely as Zechariah Frankel had conceived his mission as the building of a bridge that would reunify the factional groups among Jews, the members of the Historical School were motivated by a desire to bring about a reunion under the banner of an evolutionary concept of Judaism. The procedures that members of this school advised might even be considered analogous to the methods of science. For the mass of traditionary material that an inquirer brought with him into any question concerning innovation could be conceived as corresponding to the accumulated body of information and hypotheses that a student of any science brings with him into a new inquiry or a new phase of inquiry. On the basis of the material thus carried forward the data of the immediate situation can be interpreted and the best course of action predicted. As long as we possibly can, we hold as closely as we can to the guidance supplied by this funded body of knowledge; only when it leads us grossly astray are we pressed to a radical reconsideration of fundamentals. Thus all the warm comforts of traditionalism can be retained, without the lapse into irrelevancy and inconsequentiality that so often accompanies traditionalism. And gradual adaptation and innovation in beliefs and practices can be achieved, without the fall into rootlessness and anomie that so often accompanies innovation. The practice of the positive sciences themselves is the best illustration of the sort of adaptive traditionalism, and cautious and conservative radicalism, advocated by the Historical School.

If, however, the intention of the Historical School to reunify the Jews of the United States were to be achieved, it could no longer be, as Leeser had hoped it might, on the basis of a common religious uniformity. The unity would have to be one that transcended differences in the interpretation of Judaism, and that recognized the right to differ in belief, and even in practice, as a fundamental right of the Jew. Historical Judaism had to interpret the history of Judaism as a democratic history in order to justify its own in-

clusiveness. By implication at least, if not explicitly, this
meant that the Historical School, largely composed of rabbis,
took a position that undermined the traditional authority of
the rabbinate. The idea of a body of elite interpreters, de-
scended in a direct line of oral transmission from Moses on
Mount Sinai, had to give place to the idea of a body of sensitive spokesmen for the sentiments of the mass of the Jewish
people. The totality of Israel (*Klal Yisrael*), sometimes translated as "Catholic Israel," became the watchword of the
Historical School. The reinstitution of the Jewish community, in some form, became a major objective of their work.
All Jews, regardless of their "party" affiliations, shared in the
millennial Jewish tradition, had a common concern for the
fate of Jewry in the present age, and bore a responsibility
for the transmission and preservation of Judaism in the future. Historical continuity itself is the factor transcending
contemporary divergences and, therefore, the constitutive
principle of the Jewish community.[11]

Whether or not there was a theoretical warrant for such a
conception of the Jewish community, it was true that Jewish
community organization in the United States on any more
than a local basis arose out of the common concern of the
Jews of America for their brethren in other parts of the
world rather than out of shared religious ideas. The reaction
of the Jews of America to the suffering of the Jews of Damascus in the aftermath of the "blood libel" of 1840 was in-
stantaneous, unified, and, within limits, effective. The actions
taken by the Jews signify the coming to self-consciousness of
the American Jewish group—not yet a community.[12] The
protests by American Jews, after 1851, of a proposed Swiss-
American treaty that would have sanctioned discrimination
against American Jews in some parts of Switzerland is another instance of group action of a pre-communal nature.[13]
Formal organization arose in consequence of yet another incident, the Mortara case, in Italy, in 1858 and 1859.

A Jewish child had been secretly baptized some years

earlier by his Christian nurse, of course without the consent of the child's parents. The authorities then took the child from his parents and put him in a foster home where he would receive a Catholic education. Jewish groups in both Europe and America, when this shocking affair became public, were vocal in their protests. In both the Damascus Affair and the case of the Swiss-American Treaty, the protests of the Jews of the United States were influential in determining the position taken by their government. In the Mortara case, to the deep disappointment of all, the protest had no influence. President Buchanan declined to intervene on the specious ground that he had not been President when the incident occurred. The true reason probably was that he did not wish to establish a precedent of interfering in the affairs of another nation. The heads of other states felt no such compunction; both Napoleon III of France and Franz Josef II of Austria made ineffectual representations to the pope, Pius IX, then still the secular ruler of Bologna where the outrage had taken place.[14]

The Jews of both France and the United States, however, learned from the Mortara case the desirability of national organization. The Jews of England had had such an organization, the Board of Deputies of British Jews, since the eighteenth century. After the Mortara case, the French Jews, under the leadership of Adolphe Crémieux, organized the Alliance Israélite Universelle.[15] The American Jews, stung into the realization that they, too, needed a permanent body to represent Jewish interests, moved into preliminary steps that led, ultimately, to the establishment of The Board of Delegates of American Israelites. It was, appropriately, in Philadelphia that the very first move toward national organization took place, two resolutions being adopted by the Executive Committee of the Philadelphia Israelites. The first of these expressed regret at the rebuff by the President and affirmed that if the protest had come from the Jews of the entire nation, in the form of petitions with thousands of

signatures, instead of coming independently from the separate Jewish communities, the result would have been more
satisfactory. The second resolution recommended that congregations throughout the country consider "the propriety of
electing delegates to represent them in future, so as to form
a body similar to the Board of Deputies of British Jews in
London. For united, we can accomplish almost everything;
otherwise, nothing." [16]

The actual organizational steps were begun by Samuel
Isaacs, editor of the *Jewish Messenger* and minister of Congregation Shaaray Tefila in New York City. Through his
agency, in 1859, his congregation issued an invitation to all
other congregations in the United States to attend a meeting
to develop a plan "for the establishment of a Board of Representatives of the Israelites of the United States." [17] As a
result, late in 1859, the Board of Delegates of American
Israelites was organized by forty-six representatives of twenty-
five congregations in fourteen cities,

> to gain statistical information, to promote education and litera-
> ture, to further the cause of charity, to watch over occurrences at
> home and abroad relating to the Israelites, and to establish a
> "Court of Arbitration" for the settlement of disputes between
> Congregations, etc. without recourse to litigation.[18]

Like Isaacs himself, the rabbis who fostered this organization
were adherents of the middle way, and the congregations that
participated were mostly describable as moderate and traditional. Reform leaders were generally critical. Isaac M. Wise
wrote several pieces in his *American Israelite* indicating his
belief that the Board of Delegates was too closely tied to the
Jewish life of the eastern seaboard. David Einhorn, speaking
for the more radical wing of Reform Judaism, argued that
Jews as Jews should not come before the American public,
but that they should register their views as citizens of the
United States. He maintained, in addition, that the Board
of Delegates was a covert attempt to establish a controlling
authority over the lives and the religious practices of the

Jews of the entire country. Because of the abstention of Reform leaders from participation in its foundation, the major share of the credit for this first national Jewish organization in America must be assigned to the Historical School. Within two decades, however, the Board of Delegates was controlled by the Union of American Hebrew Congregations, the action arm of the Reform movement. The members of the Historical School found themselves without an organ for the expression of their viewpoint and were driven to new constructive efforts.[19]

## THE EMERGENCE OF THE CONSERVATIVE MOVEMENT

As a Historical School, this group of rabbinical and lay leaders maintained, as we have seen, the concept of the "Totality of Israel." They hoped to be able to establish Jewish institutions in the United States that would be inclusive, that would mediate between the extreme positions of the Reformers and the adherents of Orthodoxy. Their objective was to reunify the Jews, torn by the strife of decades, around a program for action, rather than an ideology. In this hope they were disappointed. They were able to achieve some measure of cooperation with the Orthodox group, when the target was some of the more radical proposals of the Reformers or when, as in the case of the Hebrew Union College "shrimp banquet," Orthodox views and those of the Historical School were equally offended.[20] They were able to cooperate with the Reform movement in welfare activities and in resistance to newly developing anti-Semitic trends in the American Christian public and to a stepped-up missionary campaign. The mass immigration of Eastern European Jews in this period was a major factor in the increase of anti-Semitism; it was also the source of the chief need for relief activities. At this time, too, occurred one of the periodic attempts to destroy the American tradition of freedom of religion by amending the Constitution to declare Christianity the religion of the land.[21] Against this drive the Reformers and the members of the Historical School were firmly united.

On more fundamental matters and basic principles, however, there was no union. The Reform Movement, in the view of the Historical School, had gone too far in its rejection of rabbinic Judaism and the customs and traditions of centuries of Jewish living; the Orthodox, even the Neo-Orthodox, were still too exclusively dominated by the sixteenth-century synthesis of Jewish law, the *Shulhan Arukh* of Joseph Karo, to be comfortable in association with the Historical School. It became evident that only a third force in American Judaism could adequately meet the religious needs of those who sought a middle way. So, while continuing cooperative activities in those areas where they were possible, the rabbis of the Historical School began, shortly before 1880, to move toward what was ultimately to become that third force, the Conservative Movement, in the American-Jewish scene. The necessity for such a move became clear to all after the Reform rabbis had formulated the Pittsburgh Platform of 1885 under the influence of the radical thinking of Kaufmann Kohler.

The nascent Conservative Movement began in the recognition that the Reform protest against the domination of Jewish life by Karo's codification was largely justified. During the earlier period of rabbinic activity, and especially during the period in which the Talmud was being formed, there was a rabbinical authority in permanent existence with the power, according to Jewish tradition, to interpret the law in terms of current conditions. Since Karo's *Shulhan Arukh* the dead letter of the book had replaced the live authority of the rabbinical synod. Change was correspondingly more difficult, yet the need for change was, if anything, far more acute. The ultimate hope of the conservative rabbis was that the rabbinical synod could be reorganized on a world basis. Until this restoration of synodical authority could take place, they favored an effort to restore as much of traditional practice as possible by leading the Jews of

America in a program to encourage sabbath observance; to stimulate increased attention to the following of the dietary laws; to strengthen Jewish education, especially in respect to the centrality of the Hebrew language; and to support re-settlement in Palestine. Thus, although the transitional group soon to form the nucleus of the Conservative Move-ment accepted the Reform diagnosis of the ills of traditional Judaism, the therapy it proposed was totally different.

A new American-Jewish periodical, the *American Hebrew,* became the journalistic voice of the new school. In editorial after editorial the *American Hebrew* presented the case for the convening of a new rabbinical synod:

The true want of the age is a recognized religious authority, which shall obviate all fear of head and neck change, we mean not the exaltation of a man, whose will shall be law, no Jewish Pope, far from it—but we ask for a periodical synod of the Jewish clergy, to consider the advance of the times and the change of thought, to decide what customs are obsolete, what innovations are desirable; to speak with a voice which shall ring through the Jewish world, because of the fact of its being the united voices of the renowned ministers of our faith in Europe and in America.[22]

Not even the most orthodox of our brethren will deny that many beneficial changes can be instituted in the rabbinical rules— provided a tribunal of acknowledged competency and authority be organized to consider and advise these changes. And did we not so sorely lack men of character, ability and disinterested conservatism among our American Rabbanim, the United States would be the place of places to assemble such a convention. New problems can here be worked out on a new field unhampered by ancient interests and the American solution would by force of example soon become world-spread.[23]

Even when the *American Hebrew* presented the case for or-ganization of the total Jewish community, transcending the voluntary and autonomous institutions that were then pro-liferating, its editors' argument had, ultimately, a religious and not merely a communal purpose.

Some of the innovations that had made their way in the

Reform synagogues were completely acceptable to supporters of the new movement; others could be tolerated in a modified form; still others occasioned much debate among the conservatives themselves. Thus, for example, the Reform demand for a more decorous and more esthetically pleasing service was accepted by the conservatives, in general, but they did not feel that it was necessary to go as far as the Reformers had in rejecting traditional forms in order to achieve the goal of a more "modern" service. They did not give up the use of the prayer shawl (*tallit*), because they held that its use remained meaningful, but they did tend to eliminate the special women's gallery in the synagogue and to copy the Reform pattern of family pews. They did include English translations of some of the prayers and, wherever possible, English sermons. On the matter of synagogue music, however, opinion was less uniform. There was general agreement that cantors should be more thoroughly trained musically, so that their part of the services could be carried out with more dignity. The matter of using an organ in the synagogue introduced a split between those a little to the left of Orthodoxy, who remained adamant in opposition to the introduction of organ music, and those a little to the right of Reform, who did permit the use of organ music during their services. The Reform synagogues had used choral music, with professional choirs, some of whose members were not Jewish; the conservatives accepted the idea of having a choir, but were unwilling to sanction the hiring of Christian singers. As far back as the 1820s Congregation Shearith Israel of New York City had experimented with a choir composed of young male members of the synagogue.[24] Now, under the stimulus of Rabbi H. P. Mendes, this synagogue trained a children's choir to participate in its services. Despite the desire for a strong uniformity of policy, the rabbis and their congregations went along only so far as suited their convenience or their views.[25]

Probably the single most important factor in the crystallization of the Conservative Movement was the controversy, conducted on a very high plane, between Alexander Kohut, who came to the United States as rabbi of Congregation Ahavath Chesed in New York City in 1885, and Kaufmann Kohler, an outstanding spokesman for radical Reform. Kohut's first sermon was, in effect, the program for a third force, open to orderly change but committed to the principle of interpretation of tradition as the method of change:

Is Judaism definitely closed for all time, or is it capable of and in need of continuous development? I answer both Yes and No. I answer Yes, *because religion has been given to man;* and as it is the duty of man to grow in perfection as long as he lives, he must modify the forms which yield him religious satisfaction, in accordance with the spirit of the times. I answer No, in so far as it concerns the Word of God, which cannot be imperfect. . . .

Our religious guide is the Torah, the Law of Moses, interpreted and applied in the light of tradition. But inasmuch as individual opinion cannot be valid for the whole community, it behooves individuals and communities to appoint only recognized authorities as teachers; such men, that is to say, as acknowledge belief in authority, and who, at the same time, with comprehension and tact, are willing to consider what may be permitted in view of the exigencies of the times, and what may be discarded, without changing the nature and character of the foundations of the faith. . . .

A reform which seeks to progress without the Mosaic-rabbinical tradition is a deformity—a skeleton without flesh and sinew, without spirit and heart. . . . We desire a Judaism full of life. . . . Only a Judaism true to itself and its past, yet receptive of the ideas of the present, accepting the good and the beautiful from whatever source it may come, can command respect and recognition. . . .

I do not know whether it will be my good fortune to have your sympathy in my religious attitude—that of Mosaic-rabbinical Judaism, freshened with the spirit of progress, a Judaism of the healthy golden mean. . . .[26]

Kohler, in his reply, stressed the "universal prophetic-messianic ideal" as Reform's guide, in opposition to the particularism of Kohut's "Mosaic-rabbinical Judaism." But more

important than any published reply by Kohler was the call
he issued to his fellow Reform rabbis to the Pittsburgh meeting of 1885, at which the celebrated Platform was given to
the world as a statement of the position of a large number of
leaders of the Reform Movement.[27]

After about thirty years, during which rabbis adhering to
the Historical School had cooperated, wherever possible,
with Reformed and Orthodox colleagues and institutions and
had found, ultimately, that this cooperation could be only a
very limited affair, the time had come for action and for
formal organization of the Conservative Movement. Alexander Kohut, who had supplied the final impetus by his
statement of a program, was not fitted by temperament to
take over the role of organizer. He remained the thoughtful
intellectual leader, but the practical work of organizing the
Jewish Theological Seminary of America, the first institution
of the organized Conservative Movement, fell to the lot of
the aging Sabato Morais. The Seminary began its work in
January of 1887. At the opening exercises Alexander Kohut,
who was to serve as professor of Talmud, delivered one of
the addresses and defined the purposes of the new Seminary,
using the expression "Conservative Judaism":

In the new Seminary a different spirit will prevail, different impulses will pervade its teachings and animate its teachers. This
spirit shall be that of *Conservative Judaism,* the *conserving* Jewish impulse which will create in the pupils of the Seminary the
tendency to recognize the dual nature of Judaism and the Law;
which unites theory and practice, identifies body and the soul,
realizes the importance of both matter and spirit, and acknowledges the necessity of observing the Law as well as of studying
it.[28]

### THE EXPANSION OF CONSERVATISM

Just as the coming of age of Reform may be symbolized by
the inauguration of rabbinical training in the Hebrew Union

College, so the coming of age of Conservatism may be dated from the beginning of instruction in the Jewish Theological Seminary of America. It is true that the original founding of the Seminary was spurred on by the reaction against the 1885 Pittsburgh Platform and aided by many of the Orthodox Jews, so that the Seminary under Morais was overly dominated by anti-Reform. With but slight exaggeration it may be said that during its first fifteen years the positive program of the Seminary was swallowed up in this negative objective of counteracting the spread of the Reform Movement. When Solomon Schechter (1850–1915) came to the presidency of the Seminary in 1902, emphasis shifted to the development of the positive program of Conservative, historical Judaism, as it had been enunciated by Alexander Kohut. The earlier negative approach faded into the background.

This change of emphasis may have been, at least in part, the result of an accession of strength to Conservative ranks from the more Americanized segment of the Eastern European mass immigration. The rabbis of the Conservative group had been particularly active in the effort to ease the transition of the immigrants to their new homes and to assist wherever possible in their adjustment. This was no easy task, for between 1880 and 1900 more than half a million Jewish immigrants reached American shores, arriving, for the most part, as refugees with hardly more than the clothes on their backs and without any special training that would enable them to support themselves and their families. Very few of them spoke any English. Those who had been religious in their European homelands were troubled by the prevailing notion that America was a land of irreligion—a notion that had been sedulously fostered by many of the Eastern European rabbis, and they feared for the Jewishness of their children. Those who had been touched by antireligious currents prior to migration but were unable, because of the tighter organization of the Jewish community in Eastern Europe, to give up the traditional practices and modes of living seized the opportunity free America offered to become open back-sliders, increasing the fear of their more religious brothers for the fate of Judaism in the New World.

Some of the older and better established American Jews resented the fact that, by virtue of their bearing the label of Jews, they were inevitably associated in the public mind with the newcomers. Some of the already Americanized Jews became fearful lest the climate of American opinion should change toward them as a result of the flood of newcomers who wore their differences with a defiant pride. In Boston, Rabbi Solomon Schindler overtly attacked the new arrivals both in the press and from the platform.[29] Most of his rabbinical colleagues, however, whatever their shade of opinion, felt and confronted the challenge of the new immigration as a test of the principles of the existing Jewish group, and participated enthusiastically in efforts to help the newcomers to become part of the American scene.

Immigration, of course, was nothing new in the American context. What is important for our purpose of examining religious trends in modern Judaism is that each newly arrived group brought from its homeland its own conception of the nature of Judaism and tried to superimpose this conception upon its life in America. Each new group regarded its predecessors as little better than apostates. For a few years —their number depending upon the size of the new group, where its members settled, and how long their distribution among the population took—the little nucleus tried to retain its character as an enclave, to transplant its European mode of life almost intact. Sooner or later, however, often without the group's awareness of what was happening, the process of adjustment to the American cultural scene began. The now not-so-new group became a target of scorn for its successors, and the cycle was repeated.

Adjustment moved more rapidly in the earlier period, when the immigrants came as individuals or in family groups. It moved more slowly during the period of Eastern European immigration, when the Jewish inhabitants of a whole town might come into America together and settle in the same district in some large American city, establish a little synagogue perpetuating the name of the town from which they came, and serve as a social brake on one another. Even in this period, though it took longer for the process of Americanization to begin, ultimately it did take hold, leaving, perhaps, a handful of the oldest members of the group clucking their tongues and wondering whether they had done right in leaving their homeland fifty years earlier. Again, adjustment moved more rapidly in the case of Jews who migrated from countries in which Western ideas had already begun to spread or where the general pattern of life was closer to that in the United States. Thus, the Americanization of English, Dutch, German, and German-Polish Jews proceeded more rapidly and more steadily than the Americanization of those who came from Eastern Europe. Finally, the earlier group of migrants, because of the widespread commercial opportunities at the time of their arrival, tended to disperse through the country more rapidly than later comers, and this widespread distribution hastened the process of adjustment.

By the beginning of the twentieth century some of the immigrants who had come in the first wave of the 1880s were already sufficiently "modern" and "American" to be willing to shed some of their East European religious attitudes and to accept some modifications of the traditional patterns. They were by no means ready for the wholesale rejection of tradition that was then characteristic of Reform. Moreover, as the economic situation of this group improved, they moved away from the districts in which they had first settled into other areas in which they, or their children, came into contact with a way of life which was still Jewish, but was no longer Orthodox. In this fashion a large part of the following of Conservative Judaism came out of an Orthodox East European background. The originators of the movement had been chiefly men of Sephardic or Western European ancestry, but increasingly the membership of Conservative congregations was drawn from newer immigrant strains.

Solomon Schechter himself came of Rumanian background and had a deep appreciation of the pietistic element in Eastern European Judaism. He retained a great deal of traditionalism in his thought and in his observance, although "he was not punctilious in every detail." [30] Yet he was also thoroughly trained as a scholar in the Western European sense of the word and had held a distinguished position as Reader in Rabbinics at Cambridge University before coming to America to assume the presidency of the Seminary. He acknowledged his debt to the Enlightenment in one of his last writings, a preface to the collection, *Seminary Addresses and Other Papers,* published in the year of his death:

I still belong to that older world which accepted certain humanitarian principles handed down to us from the French Revolution as God-given truths, and which still looks upon the "Declaration of Independence," based on the same principles, as a sacred document in spite of all its "glittering generalities." These "glittering generalities" have built up the new world, while the so-called "eternal verities" or "realities" are destroying the old world.[31]

Yet he combined with this appeal to the principles of Enlightenment and with a keen sense of the "desirability of adopting in our studies all the methods which distinguish modern research from the mere erudition of olden times" a constant "plea for traditional Judaism, . . . a better appreciation of Israel's past, . . . a deeper devotion to the laws distinctly characteristic of the Jewish conception of holiness, leading to a more strict observance of the precepts of the Torah." [32]

Schechter stood on the borderline between two worlds. He retained in his thought both the negative, anti-Reform element in Conservative Judaism and a peculiarly ambivalent attitude toward Eastern European Orthodoxy. In addressing the founding meeting of the United Synagogue of America, the action arm of the Conservative Movement, in 1913, he said that the Eastern European group, "by the mere virtue of their numbers again brought the Conservative tendency into prominence"; here he used the term "Conservative" to mean no more than "traditionalist." However, he also noted this "drawback":

Coming from a part of the world where . . . any adherence to the "Intelligenzia" is almost tantamount to throwing off the yoke of the Torah and the Law, they still insist, or a large influential body among them insists, that secular education and modern methods in school and college are incompatible with Orthodox principles. . . . They have, further, also this in common with at least the first reformers in this country: that they dread the English sermon just as those reformers did, the only difference being that the latter gave the preference to German and the former to Yiddish. Unfortunately they differ from the reformers in that they have never succeeded in creating proper order and decorum in their places of worship and have, besides, shown very little ability in the art of organization, which is the great strength of our Reform brethren. These our brethren are, undoubtedly, much stronger in numbers than the Reformers. But chaos reigns supreme among them. . . . To object to strict order and decorum in our places of worship, means to expel our children from the synagogue, and to point out for them the way leading to the Ethical Culture hall and similar un-Jewish institutions.[33]

Thus there was something of an uneasy compromise between modernism and traditionalism in Schechter's thought. His version of the "middle way" shifted alternately to right and to left of center. He was, however, decisive in action, and under his leadership the Jewish Theological Seminary faculty reached a high level of competence.

As the program of the Conservative group, expressed through the Seminary and its graduates, became richer, there was developed a union of Conservative congregations, the United Synagogue of America (1913). The Rabbinical Assembly (1919) united the Conservative rabbis, chiefly graduates of the Seminary, as the Central Conference of American Rabbis (1889) brought together the Reform rabbis. Other collateral organizations were formed in the course of the years, generally duplicating the alignment of forces in the Reform movement. The Conservative way gained enormously in adherents as the twentieth century progressed. Its organization developed in complexity and in stability. One reason for its popular success may very well be its failure to achieve precise definition of its position on either ritual or legal questions. As Cyrus Adler, one of the guiding lights of the early days of the Conservative Movement, explained, "Conservative is a general term which nearly everybody uses but which is, I believe, technically applied to those congregations which have departed somewhat in practice from the Orthodox, but not to any great extent in theory." [34] To this we might add Solomon Schechter's comment that the American-born second generation of Jews "accept all the ancient ideas, but they want modern methods, and this, on the whole, may be the definition of Conservative Judaism." [35]

SOME COMPLEXITIES OF CONSERVATIVE JUDAISM

Thus far, it is clear that the rabbinical and scholarly leaders of the Conservative Movement had a theoretical orientation that differs from Orthodoxy in the degree to which it accepts the absolute authority of Joseph Karo's sixteenth-century codification of Jewish Law in the *Shulhan Arukh*. The earlier stages of Conservative Judaism were, perhaps, marked more by the attempt to counter the successes of the Reform Movement than by the effort to distinguish its position from that of Orthodoxy. In consonance with this anti-Reform impulse, Conservative rabbis made minor modifications in the traditional ritual of the synagogue service and minor concessions to "Westernization" and "modernization," such as the introduction of English sermons, the confirmation of girls as well as the *bar mitzvah* (traditional initiation of boys), and, in some cases, the substitution of family pews for the traditional separation of men and women during worship. By making concessions in these matters, even as the Reform Movement had done, the early leaders hoped to be able to hold the loyalty especially of the young Americanized Jew to other aspects of the tradition.

To look at Conservative Judaism in America from the standpoint of its leading scholarly expositors is, however, to get a distorted view. It is the laity to whom we must turn to find out what Conservative Judaism really means, because much of the impulse to the development of a Conservative organization came from the laity and because (apart from the Seminary and its offshoot, the Rabbinical Assembly) Conservative Judaism has been dominated by the ideas and the motivations of its lay members. Indeed, that this lay dominance should have developed may be due to the prevalence among the scholars and rabbis of adherence to the theory of "Catholic Israel" (*klal yisrael*). Schechter, for example, wrote: "The norm as well as the sanction of Judaism is the practice actually in vogue. Its consecration is the consecration of general use, or, in other words, of Catholic Israel," [36] and added, in another place, "The Torah is not in heaven. Its interpretation is left to the conscience of Catholic Israel." [37] On the surface, at least, especially when combined with Schechter's own pleas for "democracy" in the synagogues, such expressions suggest that "Judaism" in any age is what "Jews" are willing to do and to believe. Schechter probably meant no such simplistic conception, but we should hardly be surprised to learn that others understood his meaning less subtly than he intended, or that lay dominance should be taken as a corollary of expressions like these.

What, then, is the meaning of Conservative Judaism to its laity? In the first place, it is an identification that can be maintained in consonance with other identifications. The members of Conservative congregations basically identify with middle-class American values, one of which is membership in a religious organization. The Orthodox synagogue retains behavior patterns which, in America, are identified as lower-class, though they may not have been so in the time and place of their origin. The Reform synagogues, permitting middle-class identification, provide a less satisfactory sense of Jewish identification, especially for those whose family background and upbringing was within Eastern European Orthodoxy. The Conservative Jewish identification is, if the distinction may be allowed, more ethnic than religious. It emphasizes a feeling of "Jewishness" rather than a practice of Judaism. Certain customs tend to be stressed as evidences of "Jewishness" while others, equally grounded in tradition, are disregarded. A special aura of sanctity attaches to food customs and dietary laws, probably because of their association with childhood. In the homes of many members of Conservative congregations some of the dietary laws are observed, while others are disregarded; many who maintain fairly strict observance in their homes make no pretense of conforming to the dietary laws when they eat in restaurants or in the homes of others. There is a high percentage of holiday observance and far less Sabbath observance. Hebrew schooling, to some degree, for childen is felt to be virtually obligatory, but the participation of the parents in Jewish cultural activities is far less common.[38]

The individual variation in the extent of adherence to the standards of traditional practice is very wide. So, too, is the variation from synagogue to synagogue within the Conservative Movement. Some thirty years ago a committee of the Rabbinical Assembly conducted a survey of ritual practice from which a keen sense of the diversity can be gained. Congregations that reported the use of a uniform prayer book for Sabbath services listed nine different prayer books, including the one developed by the Reform Movement. Fifteen congregations reported that they did not use a uniform prayer book. Of the 110 congregations that reported, 95 had late Friday evening services; 23 of these had *only* the late service, having abandoned the traditional early service. Some of the congregations that had followed Reform in adopting the late Friday evening service did not include any prayers, "but hymns, a review of Jewish Current Events, reading from Yiddish current literature, a lecture followed by a discussion." Special account of American patriotic occasions (Lincoln's Birthday, Thanksgiving Day, etc.) was taken by 21 congregations by means of prayers incorporated in the Friday night services preceding these patriotic holidays. Congregational reports on the Sabbath morning service noted the elimination of some of the Hebrew prayers and the reading of others in English. In some cases an English explanation of the weekly reading from the Torah was inserted into the service either directly before or directly after the reading itself. Some reported that the reading of the prophetic portion for the week (*haftarah*) was in English rather than Hebrew. Despite the cuts in the traditional service there were comments that the service was overlong. From some rabbis came objections to the "cantor idolatry" prevailing in their congregations. Considering the historical background of the Conservative Movement, the most amazing comment in the entire report was that of a rabbi who wrote that "the Torah reading is a bore which disrupts the service and has little real benefit."

As an expedient for taking care of the religious needs of the children without sacrifice of the decorum of the adult services, 78 of the congregations had instituted "junior congregations." There was, however, no consistency in the way in which these junior congregations were organized, their services conducted, and their work integrated with that of the adult congregations. Many changes in the *bar mitzvah* ceremonies were noted, including the transfer of the ceremonies from Sabbath morning to Friday night, as an accommodation to non-Sabbath-observing friends and relatives of the confirmands. A few congregations, at that time, had introduced a parallel ceremony of initiation for girls (*bat mitzvah*), marking the changed status of the female in the American cultural

environment. In addition, 81 of the Conservative synagogues
reported that they had an annual confirmation exercise, at
the celebration of *Shevuoth* (the Feast of Weeks), as a supplement to the traditional individual confirmation.

Approximately one third of the reporting congregations
no longer maintained the traditional daily services. The importance of the so-called *"Yizkor*-Jew" (one whose only relation with the synagogue was the observance of the annual
memorial rites for his parents) is evidenced by the fact that
several of the congregations that, as a general practice, had
abandoned daily services occasionally restored these services
for the sake of these sporadic observers, "when members have
*Yahrzeit.*" Many synagogues said that memorial services
(*Yizkor*) on the holidays had been transferred to the very end
of the proceedings, because otherwise, "Immediately after the
*Yizkor* services on the festivals there is a general exodus from
the Synagogue. . . . In spite of exhortations by the rabbis,
people come just in time for *Yizkor* and leave immediately
after." Some other divergences, both from traditional practice
and from the practice of other Conservative synagogues, were
noted. A few synagogues held Sunday morning services, although the nineteenth-century Reform synagogue's practice
of transferring the chief service of the week to Sunday morning had been one of Reform's major crimes in the eyes of
early Conservatives; 28 synagogues had organs and 15 of these
used the organs at Sabbath and holiday services.[39]

Similar variations can be noted in the Conservative approaches to Jewish law. A resolution of the United Synagogue
of America, sent to the Rabbinical Assembly and read at its
1931 convention, included this statement of the Conservative
attitude to Jewish law: "Let it become known once and for
all that we stand firmly on the rock of Jewish tradition and
Jewish law,—but let it also become known that we . . . seek
the lenient view, the liberal view, if you will, and not the
severe view in Jewish tradition." [40] Yet at the joint conven-

tion of the United Synagogue and the Rabbinical Assembly in 1948, the keynote speaker, Rabbi Morris Adler, said:

American Judaism, if it is to enrich the lives of Jews, must be inextricably related to the conditions and circumstances of our society. . . . No gradual and slow process of interpretations will suffice to evolve a Judaism compatible with our needs. . . . In such spheres of Jewish law as Sabbath, dietary law, laws relating to the problem of the *agunah,* we cannot any longer be content with revisions by the strict, slow process of law.[41]

In these two passages there is a reversal of roles. For the most part, until recently it has been the Conservative laity that has spoken for change and the rabbis who have held back. Here, in respect to Jewish law, the lay statement stands "firmly on the rock of Jewish tradition and Jewish law," while the rabbinical speaker urges a far more radical approach.

This may be more understandable in the light of the special question that was agitating the Conservative rabbinate in 1948, soon after the end of World War II. This was the problem of the *agunah*—the presumptive widow whose status cannot be established by testimony that the rabbinical tradition considered adequate, as when her husband is reported missing in action during a war. She is, therefore, traditionally prohibited from remarrying. Clearly some change was urgently needed. The Rabbinical Assembly held a Conference on Jewish Law in 1948, with special reference to the problem of the *agunah*. The discussion centered on the question of where, in American Jewry, there was an authority competent to make the changes that all the participants knew were necessary. The consensus of the rabbinical meeting was that, pending the establishment of a "Jewish Academy" with authority to resolve areas of conflict between present-day needs and traditional Jewish law, the best that could be done was to interpret the existing law leniently. Thus the rabbis returned to a reactionary stand, in spite of the radicalism of Adler's statement, bearing out Milton Steinberg's sharp criticism of his colleagues:

The leaders and official agencies of Conservatism have failed to live up to their preachments. Affirming tradition *and* progress, they have in half a century failed to commend a single departure, no matter how slight, from old patterns. For all practical purposes they might as well have been Orthodox.[42]

The breadth of the areas demonstrating the inconsistencies of statement and practice in Conservative Judaism makes clear that it is an adaptation peculiarly fitted for survival in a pluralistic environment. Somewhere within the complex phenomenon of Conservative Judaism any person who wishes to identify himself with the Jewish people can find a position blending tradition and innovation in precisely the proportions acceptable to him. Thus Conservatism, with all its backings and fillings, its avoidance of dogmatic positions, its uneasy balance of lay and rabbinical elements, its pragmatic character, may have supplied precisely the compromise position, the broad middle of the road needed to offset the broad, middle-of-the-road conditions faced by Judaism in twentieth-century America.

# 5

# Zionism: From Religious Nationalism to National Religion

## "A WONDROUS CALL"

In the year 586 before the Christian Era, Babylonian armies defeated the forces of Judah. Many of the inhabitants of the land were exiled into the land of the conquerors. The Temple at Jerusalem was destroyed; its ceremonies and sacrifices were abandoned. Had the course of other histories been repeated, the religion of the Hebrew people would have come to an end. This did not happen; instead, the religion was transformed. Precisely when and by whom this transformation was accomplished, we do not know. It is clear, however, that Judaism, the religion of the Jewish people, based upon a foundation of earlier Hebrew religion, was a creation of the period of the Babylonian Exile. The newly reborn religion revised the older conception of God, now no longer as the God of *a* nation, but as the God of *all* nations, whose power is universal and who uses every people as an instrument of his providential purpose. It replaced the older Hebrew conception of divine service as sacrificial ritual by a new conception of divine service as study of the Word of God

as contained in the Torah. It substituted the idea of "a kingdom of priests and a holy nation" for that of a nation divided
by a rigid caste system into priests, "Levites," and Israelites.
And it provided food for hope in a miraculous return to the
homeland and the restoration of political independence under the leadership of the "anointed one" of God, the Messiah.
Once the hope of restoration had been realized, whether as
the result of "a wondrous call" [1] or as a consequence of the
tactics of empire in that age, it could only be regarded as a
fulfilled prophecy.

Whenever at a later time of trouble and distress (of which
there were many in the history of the Jewish people) the
situation of the Jews seemed hopeless, the old fulfillment
was remembered and the cry rose once more to Heaven for
supernatural aid in restoring the older situation. After A.D.
70, when the Temple was again destroyed, by the Romans,
and the Jews dispersed through the known world, the prayer
for the Messiah, with political overtones, became a permanent
feature of Jewish life. Preachers in the synagogues invariably
concluded their addresses with a formula invoking the miraculous Redeemer: the most sacred service of the year, on the
Day of Atonement, ended with the words "Next year in
Jerusalem!" Prayers for restoration were incorporated into
every Jewish service. Religion and nationality were so welded
together that it became impossible to separate the spiritual
elements from the political. For all its universality, Judaism
developed as a religious nationalism.

At no time did Jewish habitation in Palestine completely
cease. Moreover, during the middle ages, even when travel
was extremely difficult and dangerous, many pious Jews left
their homelands to spend their last years in the Holy Land.
To die there and be buried in the sacred soil was the hope
that led them to undergo the hazards of the way. Others,
unable to go to Palestine, cherished a handful of soil brought
from the Holy Land on which their heads could be pillowed
in their graves in the lands of their exile. At no time was the

dream of restoration completely lost; the Jews continued to await the coming of the Messiah. Occasionally there arose a claimant able to convince some of the Jews that he was indeed the anointed one. Jewish history is studded with pseudo Messiahs; all of them had followers, because when the need is great the promptings of hope are stronger than the cautions of criticism. The Jews in dispersion never abandoned the idea of Palestine as their homeland; and it was the actual, the real land of which they dreamed.

For two reasons it is important to emphasize that the Jewish Messianic hope had political restoration to an actual Palestine as its goal. One is that some Jewish writers in speaking about the Land used such exaggerated language that it is hard for us to believe they had the actual country in mind. Such, for example, were the views of the Holy Land presented by the medieval poet-philosopher, Jehudah Halevi (*ca.* 1080–*ca.* 1145), who conceived that the very air of the Holy Land was imbued with a spirit of holiness and divine inspiration. Thus he accounted for the frequency of prophetic inspiration when the Jews were living in Palestine. "No other place," he wrote, "would share the distinction of the divine influence, just as no other mountain might be able to produce good wine." [2] Jehudah Halevi was describing what he thought to be the real Palestine, although his love for Zion was so rapturous as to lead him into these extreme claims. His longing to reach that real Palestine impelled him to leave Spain late in life to go there; here history loses sight of him, though legend, appropriately, speaks of his death, when pierced by the spear of an Arab horseman, at the gates of Jerusalem.

A second reason for stressing the political character of Jewish Messianism is that for the most part, when "restorationism" was adopted by non-Jews, the "Zion" of their expectations was a "heavenly Zion," not an earthly one. Many Christian writers, from the earliest days, considered the theme of restoration; its biblical roots were, after all, as much part of the Christian heritage as of the Jewish. But Christian "restorationism" was altogether a spiritual theory, generally related to the conversion of the Jews, with no political admixture. William Blake's "Jerusalem" was an ideal, not an actual city, and he pledged incessant effort to build this ideal "in England's green and pleasant land." Thomas Burnet's concern was for the "state of the Jews in the millennium, or the future kingdom of the Messiah." Burnet specifically denied that millenarian conditions could be achieved by political means. John Milton spoke of restoration as the consequence of "a wondrous call." Indeed, in every period in Christian history in which millennialist pressures were strong, the themes of apocalyptic restoration of the Jews were much discussed, and at such times Christian interest in the Jews rose to a peak. This was the case in the mid-seventeenth century, when Christian interest in the Jewish pseudo Messiah, Shabbetai Zevi (1626–76), was almost as great as Jewish interest. It was again the case in the Napoleonic period, when the upheaval of empires bore the signs, to the pious, of the preparation described in the Bible for the last period of history, the Messianic age.[3]

Whatever the Christian view, to the Jews the return to Zion was a political concept that lay at the heart of their religious attitudes and beliefs. Even when alternative, remedial schemes were proposed, they were recognized as merely temporary expedients, alleviating the Jewish situation while waiting for the return. So, in the most grandiose of these schemes, when Mordecai Manuel Noah (1785–1851) proposed to create a Jewish colony called "Ararat" on Grand Island in the Niagara River, with the hope of incorporating this Jewish commonwealth into the United States of America, his dedicatory address made clear to all that he had not abandoned the traditional view of the return:

In calling the Jews together under the protection of the American Constitution and laws and governed by our happy and salutary institutions, it is proper for me to state that this asylum is temporary and provisionary. The Jews never should and never will relinquish the just hope of regaining possession of their ancient heritage.[4]

Because restoration, in the Jewish mind, had this double aspect, both political and religious, both natural and supernatural, both human and divine, Jewish activity to bring about restoration was not limited to prayer for supernatural intervention. Resettlement and colonization schemes, once the Jews of Europe and America were in a position to plan and execute them, were as fitting as prayers.[5]

ZION AND EMANCIPATION

Centuries of oppression, hardship, and persecution failed to diminish this religio-political attachment of the Jews to the Holy Land. A few short years of kindness and acceptance in Western Europe, in the context of Enlightenment and emancipation, weakened the attachment almost to the point of disappearance. Among the followers of Moses Mendelssohn the demand that the "creed" of Judaism be reformulated to accord with the principles of reason carried in its train a call for the reexamination of the conception of a separate Jewish nationality. To the extent that the new order in Europe involved at least a partial emancipation of the Jews, it was especially important that the Napoleonic question concerning the national loyalties of the Jews receive a clear-cut answer: "Do those Jews who are born in France and who are treated as French citizens regard France as their native country, and do they feel themselves obligated to defend it, to obey its laws, and to submit to all regulations of the civil code?" [6] Substitute Germany, Holland, England, the United States for France in this question: it is the question that the age of emancipation had to ask; it is the question that the Jews of that age had to answer. The answer of Western European Jewry was to turn its back on the age-old fusion of political and religious elements in the Messianic dream and to separate the religious and national aspects of Judaism.

In part, the transformation is to be understood as a change from thinking about Judaism as a religious nationalism to thinking about the Jews as a religious community. A clear expression of this new way of thinking is to be seen in the ideas of the German Reform leader, Ludwig Philippson:

Formerly [the Jews] had striven to create a nation, an independent state, but now their goal was to join other nations and reach for the highest rung of development in human society. It was the task of the new age to form a general human society which would encompass all peoples organically. In the same way, it was the task of the Jews not to create their own nation and their own state or a separate political entity, but rather to obtain from the other nations full acceptance into their society and thereby attain to participation in the general body social.[7]

Adherence to a Jewish religious community and striving for acceptance in the "general body social" are not incompatible aims. They do not, the leaders of Western European Jewry repeatedly declared, lead to divided loyalties. David W. Marks, the first rabbi of the characteristically named West London Synagogue of British Jews, emphatically presented this viewpoint in 1845:

It is true that we look to our restoration to Judaea, but only at that time when the whole tone of society will be changed, and when all nations will be subjected to a system of government totally different from that which now obtains. But until that period arrives—and mark well it is to be attended by such wonders as are to eclipse the miracles of Egypt—we unequivocally declare that we neither seek nor acknowledge subjection to any land except the land of our birth. To this land we attach ourselves with a patriotism as glowing, with a devotion as fervent, and with a love as ardent and sincere as any class of our British non-Jewish fellow citizens.[8]

There is no incompatibility between national political loyalties and religious acceptance of the doctrine of miraculous restoration.

Abraham Geiger, in his Hegelian treatment of the doctrine of the "Chosen People," contributed an interestingly paradoxical reading of the theme of Judaism as a religious community. Throughout Jewish history, he said, there has been a tension in the Jewish mind between its sense of nationality, leading to such claims as that the Jews are God's "Chosen People," and its sense of universal message and mission. In this respect, the Jews are not unique; every people goes through a similar course of development. At some time in its history every people finds its own particularism in conflict with a sense of universal destiny generated by concentration on its own particular qualities. Where Judaism is unique, for Geiger, is that, over the centuries, it has worked its way through this polarity to a point where the sense of nationality has yielded completely to the sense of universality. "Judaism has proved itself a force outliving its peculiar nationality, and therefore may lay claim to special consideration." [9] The implication of Geiger's position is that Judaism can, without loss to its own character, eliminate any residue of the older "nationalistic" phase that survives in traditional doctrinal or liturgical formulas.

Views such as these required a reconsideration and reformulation of the theological treatment of Jewish dispersion. No longer could theologians consistently assert that the dispersion was a punishment for Israel's sins, to be ended when God was satisfied with the genuineness and sincerity of Israel's repentance. The negative understanding of dispersion gave way to a positive understanding, according to which dispersion was a necessary step in the fulfillment of Israel's mission. Thus Samuel Holdheim could say,

It is the destiny of Judaism to pour the light of its thoughts, the fire of its sentiments, the fervor of its feelings upon all souls and hearts on earth. Then all of these peoples and nations, each according to its soil and historic characteristics, will, by accepting our teachings, kindle their own lights, which will then shine independently and warm their souls. Judaism shall be the seed-bed of the nations filled with blessing and promise, but not a fully grown matured tree with roots and trunk, crowned with branches and twigs, with blossoms and fruit—a tree which is merely to be transplanted into a foreign soil. . . . Judaism wants to purify the languages of the nations, but leave to each people its own tongue. It wishes for one heart and one soul, but not for one sound and one tone.[10]

The mission of Israel is to spread the pure ethical teachings of Judaism among the nations of the world without, at the same time, destroying the individual characters of the nations—or of Judaism.

Along with this shift in the theology of dispersion went a reinterpretation of the doctrine of the Messiah. Some Western European leaders, even among the Reformers, tried to maintain, as a purely spiritual doctrine, that in the millennial future God would send a personal Messiah to lead the new Israel in triumph back to its ancient homeland, and that Jerusalem would then be, as Ludwig Philippson expressed it, in commenting on chapter 60 of the book of Isaiah, "broadened from the capital of its nation to the capital of the whole world." Thus, in some of the early Reformers, the doctrine of the Messiah was retained, with its political implications omitted, and its universal spiritual themes emphasized.

However, we do not interpret those promises in a narrow, particularistic sense, which would have the Messiah redeem only Israel and grant it the power to rule over the rest of the world; no, indeed; we base our hope mainly on the sayings of the God-chosen prophets, in which the Messiah is assigned an infinitely greater, nobler role, namely, the salvation and redemption of all mankind, the union of all nations into one peaceful realm, to serve their one true God.[11]

For the most part, however, Reform Judaism in the nineteenth century eliminated the doctrine of the personal Messiah completely, replacing it with the conception of a Messianic age of truth, justice, and peace for all mankind. A most explicit statement of the rejection of the personal Messiah is to be found in the *Programm zu einer Erklärung deutscher Israeliten, Freunden religiöser Reform im Judenthume zur Beherzigung vorgelegt* (Program for a declaration of German Israelites, Friends of Religious Reform . . .), which appeared in 1843, the manifesto of the Frankfort Society of Friends of Reform: "A Messiah who is to lead back the Israelites to the land of Palestine is neither expected nor desired by us; we know no fatherland except that to which we belong by birth or citizenship." [12] The Rabbinical Conference at Frankfort (1845), after much discussion, endorsed an uneasy compromise: "The Messianic idea should receive prominent mention in the prayers, but all petitions for our return to the land of our fathers and for the restoration of a Jewish state should be eliminated from the prayers." [13] It remained for the Pittsburgh Platform of the American Reformers, in 1885, to deliver the strongest blow to the traditional doctrine:

We recognize, in the modern era of universal culture of heart and intellect, the approaching of the realization of Israel's great Messianic hope for the establishment of the kingdom of truth, justice, and peace among all men. We consider ourselves no longer a nation, but a religious community, and therefore expect neither a return to Palestine, nor a sacrificial worship under the sons of Aaron, nor the restoration of any of the laws concerning the Jewish state.[14]

That the Reform leaders should, under the spur of Enlightenment and in the hope of emancipation, transform the traditional teachings in this fashion is not surprising. It is, however, more striking that those who followed more traditional approaches to Judaism, in Germany at least, were also eager to find their rationale within the terms of the Enlightenment-emancipation complex. Samson Raphael Hirsch, for example, was completely ready to abandon the idea of a Jewish nationality. His interpretation of the ancient Jewish state and its territory was nonpolitical. State and territory were the physical means, merely, by which the Hebrew people could fulfil its "spiritual calling." "Land and soil," he wrote, "were never Israel's bond of union." [15] From the very beginning, Israel was held together by spiritual bonds. Consequently Hirsch, like the Reformers, could answer the basic question of the age by a firm assertion that there was no possible conflict between being a Jew and being a German. "It is our duty to join ourselves as closely as possible to the state which receives us into its midst, to promote its welfare and not to consider our wellbeing as in any way separate from that of the state to which we belong." [16] Moreover, Hirsch, again like the Reformers, talked of the mission of Israel among the nations, though he did not reconstruct the theology of dispersion—for him it was still Exile (*Galut*). The Neo-Orthodox position maintained by Hirsch lacked the consistency of the Reform position, but it was equally a response to emancipation in its separation of religious and political elements in Judaism.[17]

FORESHADOWINGS OF ZIONISM

These early spokesmen of Reform and Neo-Orthodoxy stood ready to sacrifice the nationalist element of Judaism to their desire to enter into the emancipated world. But their "defensive distinction between civic duty and religion," [18] which made religion solely responsible for Jewish survival, allows of an alternative interpretation as the basis for a non-religious Jewish nationalism. In short, Zionism, although it is surely in some historical continuity with earlier politico-religious ideas, is rather to be understood as another of the constructive attempts of Judaism in confrontation with the modern world. It is one of the ways in which "Jewish thought has been attempting to rebuild a definition of Jewish identity." [19] To understand the historical necessity for this reshaping of the nationalist element in Jewish thought, we must remember that the emancipated status that Enlightenment held out to the Jews of Western Europe never really materialized and that the Jews of Eastern Europe never shared the promise. By the time that enlightened emancipation had progressed far enough for the patterns of Jewish interpretation that I have discussed to have developed, the Western European world had already retreated from Reason and Enlightenment to a new irrationalism, a new authoritarianism, in some respects a new medievalism. This reversion is apparent as early as 1815, in the Congress of Vienna, and it certainly persists, in a wide variety of political and social forms, into our own day. At the very time, then, when such Jewish thinkers as Abraham Geiger and Samson Raphael Hirsch were working out their contrasting philosophies for emancipated Judaism, the forces that were to make these philosophies irrelevant in Europe at least—far less so in the United States of America—were already on the march. The resurgence, in the nineteenth century and after, of persecutions, pogroms, blood accusations, and "blood and soil" theories of nationalism destroyed the very conditions that had made Jewish acceptance of emancipation so easy. Thus Zionism begins in confrontation with modern irrationalism, a different aspect of the modern world from that faced by Reform and Neo-Orthodoxy.

The foreshadowings of Zionism developed in a world in which nationalism was the central and driving force. This was, of course, true of all of Europe in the mid-nineteenth century, but it was especially true of certain "buffer" areas which had long been under "foreign" sovereignty—the Balkan States and divided Poland. Zionism's forerunners were stimulated also by a keen sense of the hazardous position of the Jews as an alien element in the new world of nationalism. Yehudah Alkalai (1798–1878), for example, an almost

forgotten proto-Zionist, was born in Serbia, spent his early
years in Palestine, and returned to his native country in
1825. His return came soon after the Greek revolution
against Turkish domination had come to a successful conclusion, inspiring other Balkan national independence efforts. In this time and place his thoughts naturally turned to
the possibility of a similar effort for Jewish national independence. Although he was a rabbi of the most traditionalist stripe, Alkalai could see no objection to human effort as
preparing the ground for the later miraculous redemption.
As early as 1834 he suggested the establishment of Jewish
settlements in the Holy Land; his advocacy of self-redemption
for the Jewish people became a holy crusade after 1840, when
the Damascus blood libel persuaded him that the only way
for the Jews to earn security was by establishing a national
home in Palestine, which, he thought, could be bought or
rented from the Turkish rulers. Alkalai was nothing if not
practical:

I ask of our brethren that they organize a company, on the mode
of the fire insurance companies and of the railroad companies.
Let this company appeal to the Sultan to give us back the land
of our ancestors in return for an annual rent. Once the name of
Israel is again applied to our land, all Jews will be inspired to
help this company with all the means at their disposal. Though
this venture will begin modestly, its future will be very great.[20]

He foresaw the need for the creation of a governing authority, and went so far as to suggest that the assembly chosen
for this purpose would be the fulfillment of the prophecies
concerning the forerunner of the Messiah. Some of Alkalai's
practical suggestions have, in fact, been carried out by later
Zionist organizations.

Another traditionalist rabbi who, despite his traditionalism, was able to argue for a secular concept of return to the
Holy Land was Zvi Hirsch Kalischer (1795–1874). Kalischer
was born in Posen—German Poland—and witnessed several

unsuccessful attempts on the part of the Russian Poles, across the border, to win independence for Poland once again. In 1836 Kalischer was already convinced that "the beginning of the Redemption will come through natural causes by human effort and by the will of the governments to gather the scattered of Israel into the Holy Land." [21] He did not develop his thinking on this subject, however, until a quarter of a century later, when he joined a society to stimulate Jewish settlement in Palestine. Then he wrote, as a supplement to one of his earlier works, a book called *Derishat Zion* (Seeking Zion), which appeared in 1862. He argued here, to the consternation of some of the Orthodox rabbis of his time, that the miraculous Messiah is not necessary for the salvation of the Jews, which can occur by natural means, as self-redemption. "The Redemption of Israel, for which we long, is not to be imagined as a sudden miracle. . . . On the contrary, the Redemption will begin by awakening support among the philanthropists and by gaining the consent of the nations to the gathering of some of the scattered of Israel into the Holy Land." [22] Other Orthodox leaders were prepared to accept Kalischer's notion that the colonization of Palestine should be immediately undertaken with subsidies from wealthy Jews, perhaps because he tempered it with the suggestion that the resettlement could properly be made the occasion for the restoration of the sacrificial rituals.

Along more practical lines, Kalischer advocated the stimulation of agriculture as a means of making the Palestinian colonies he envisaged self-supporting. He added: "Another great advantage of agricultural settlement is that we would have the privilege of observing the religious commandments that attach to working the soil of the Holy Land." [23] The most important result of Kalischer's theories and his prodding of his fellows was the foundation in 1870 of the first Jewish agricultural school in Palestine, under the sponsorship of the Alliance Israélite Universelle. The extent to which Kalischer was aware of the nationalist movements in Europe in his time is well demonstrated in these words from *Derishat Zion:*

Why do the people of Italy and of other countries sacrifice their lives for the land of their fathers, while we, like men bereft of strength and courage, do nothing? Are we inferior to all other peoples, who have no regard for life and fortune as compared with the love of their land and nation? Let us take to heart the examples of the Italians, Poles, and Hungarians, who laid down their lives and possessions in the struggle for national independence, while we, the children of Israel, who have the most glorious and holiest of lands as our inheritance, are spiritless and silent. We should be ashamed of ourselves! All the other peoples have striven only for the sake of their own national honor; how much more should we exert ourselves, for our duty is to labor not only for the glory of our ancestors but for the glory of God who chose Zion! [24]

In both Alkalai and Kalischer there is a blend of Eastern European Jewish piety, with a touch of what is almost mysticism, and Western European political nationalism. Moses Hess (1812–75) came to his proto-Zionism from a different direction of nineteenth-century thought. Although his early education was in the Jewish tradition, he grew indifferent to his religious background and entered upon a career in journalism and politics. He was active, especially in the 1840s, in revolutionary socialist circles. Hess worked with Karl Marx and Friedrich Engels at this time, but his approach differed from theirs because of his unwillingness to accept the materialistic basis on which they developed their system. His own thought was far more influenced by ethical considerations and by the humanism of the romantic movement. Hess became dissatisfied with the fruits of political activism as a result of the limited outcomes of the revolutions of 1848, and retired to a life of study. His dormant Jewish consciousness had been reawakened at the time of the Damascus Affair in 1840, and after his retirement from active political engagement he devoted much of his time to a thorough reconsideration of the nature of Jewish nationalism. All the themes of his thought were brought together in a short volume called *Rome and Jerusalem* (1862), in which he went so far as to recommend that the Jews voluntarily yield their emancipated status if it conflicted with their sense of Jewish nationality.

It is clear in Hess's work that the social-democratic ideals for which he had fought as an activist remained central to his conception of Jewish nationalism. For him, "The contemporary movements for national self-realization do not only not exclude a concern for all humanity but strongly assert it." [25] Jewish nationalism, too, had in his vision an opportunity to exert its force universally. The romantic association of nation and soil loomed large in Hess's mind. He thought of a "fatherland" as a necessary precondition for all significant achievement.

The masses are never moved to progress by mere abstract conceptions; the springs of action lie far deeper than even the socialist revolutionaries imagine. With the Jews, more than with other nations which, though oppressed, yet live on their own soil, all political and social progress must necessarily be preceded by national independence. A common, native soil is a precondition for introducing healthier relations between capital and labor among the Jews. . . . The Jewish people will participate in the great historical movement of present-day humanity only when it will have its own fatherland. [26]

Hess foresaw no important objection from the nations, especially those nations then fighting for their own unification and independence, to a Jewish struggle for a national homeland. For Germany and Italy, both of which were at this time striving for unification, to deny the Jews the same right to a land of their own would be "the most fatal inconsistency." [27] Hess did not envision the return of all the Jews to Palestine. He thought that many, especially of those "who live at present in the civilized countries of the Occident will undoubtedly remain where they are." [28] The existence of a center of Jewish national life would, however, make it unnecessary to fight for naturalization and emancipation. All modern nations have both a center and dispersed members; the Jews have only the dispersed members and lack the national center. Hess hoped to remedy this deficiency and thus to make of the Jewish people, whether within the borders of the national homeland or outside of them, a modern nation and a spiritual unity.

Modern Zionism, while it still preserves elements of the older Messianic hope, involves the attempt to develop practical plans for human effort in the building of a national homeland. It gives a secular and practical turn to a religious concept of supernatural redemption. Taking Zionism in this sense, it has an American prehistory as well as a European. The millennial hopes and Messianic dreams were not completely discarded, but they were kept apart from the secular national schemes. Devotion to the Messianic ideal was demonstrated by continuing support of the small groups of mendicant Jews who lived in the Holy Land. As early as 1759 Moses Malki visited both New York and Newport as a collector of charitable gifts, and donations for the support of the Jews of Palestine were entrusted to him.[29] A series of later messengers (*meshullachim*) came to the United States, and at least two relief societies were founded before 1860.[30] There was some difference of opinion in American-Jewish circles about the desirability of this sort of contribution, because some Jews felt that the recipients of this form of charity were being encouraged to persist in their "indolence."

An extreme statement of this hostile attitude can be found in the *Jewish Times* for February 10, 1871. The writer comments on the appeals from Jerusalem:

We have no doubt they are starving there, and the hungry is entitled by right of nature to receive his bread from those who can give it. But have the majority of these people any business to be there and starve? . . . Had they employed the same amount of energy to reach a place where they could find work and employment and a proper sphere for their physical and mental energies, they would, without a doubt, be dispensers instead of receivers of alms.

As long as these pious fanatics are encouraged by other pious people, who merely lack the intensity of purpose and the courage to follow their example, they will continue to flock there. Starvation in their eyes is one of the steps to heaven. . . . That will not deter them as long as contributions pour in to alleviate their misery.

This most unsympathetic attitude toward those for whom the return to Zion was exclusively an expression of Messianic hope was not in the least unusual in nineteenth-century America. The virulence with which it is expressed is its unusual feature.

The very same attitude and ideology of work that lie behind such a criticism of those whose religious zeal led them to be willing to live as permanent pensioners on their fellow Jews may explain the hospitality of the Jews of America to resettlement and agricultural programs for Palestine. Because most of the Jews in America had entered commercial life they were especially prone to approve most heartily proposals that would siphon other Jews into agriculture. Brief reference has been made to Mordecai Manuel Noah's Ararat proposal, as a makeshift and temporary arrangement, preparatory to the restoration. Another American scheme for return was that of Warder Cresson (1798–1860), who became a convert to Judaism in 1848, assuming the name of Michael Boaz Israel. Cresson (or Israel) attempted in 1852 to set up a model farm by means of which he could "communicate any knowledge that I possess in relation to the best and most economical system of farming." [31] Thus he hoped to take the lead in a Jewish return to the soil of the Holy Land. Unfortunately the attempt failed.

Isaac Leeser, who perhaps of all the more prominent American Jews of his day might have been most expected to sympathize with the Messianic view, took his stand with the advocates of practical agricultural colonization, and was, indeed, most friendly to Cresson's proposal and attempted to gain support for it. In editorial comment in *The Occident,* after recalling to his readers the frequency with which he had brought to their attention appeals for Palestinian Jews, Leeser continued:

We need not be reminded that at present the hills are naked, stripped of the soil which once rendered them fertile. But we have read in a late publication, that they are limestone rock, and that it would not require overmuch labor, by breaking them up with spade and plough, to make them pay the husbandman's toil with plentiful crops of all kinds of farm produce. This is said to be the case even with the naked hills; but what shall we say of the fertile valleys, which now lie desolate, because there is no farming population to plant them? Other lands suffer because the population is too dense for their productiveness; but here is a spot situated in the centre of the courts of commerce, between the east and the west, weeping, so to say, because there are *too few* to satisfy its craving to nourish them. And who more than the Israelites have a claim on the soil of Palestine to obtain therein their support? Who, more than we, are better calculated to draw the full benefit of Nature's bountiful gifts in our ancient patrimony? Many nations have borne sway over it; but it has not responded with its healthful products to their desire.[32]

Not a word of miraculous redemption or of a supernatural Messiah did Leeser include, even as a sop, in this editorial. He was strictly concerned with the idea of establishing agricultural colonies for stability and prosperity, and "to restore . . . an honorable feeling of self-dependence and self-support, and . . . to do away with the necessity of constantly appealing for alms to feed starving thousands in our ancient patrimony." [33]

In Eastern Europe, too, especially after the pogroms of the 1880s, the proto-Zionist concept of a secular return found stirring voices. Peretz Smolenskin (1842–85) had developed a theory of Jewish cultural nationalism even before the pogroms; after them he modified his theory to call for the complete abandonment of Eastern Europe by Jews and their resettlement in Zion. In the 1870s Smolenskin struggled for the conception of the Jews as a "spiritual nation," bound together by the tie of the Torah.

We have never ceased being a people, even after our kingdom was destroyed and we were exiled from our land, and whatever may yet come over us will not eradicate our national character. But we are not today a people like all others, just as we were not a people like the others even when we dwelt in our own land. The foundation of our national identity was never the soil of the Holy Land, and we did not lose the basis of our nationality when we were exiled. We have always been a spiritual nation, one whose Torah was the foundation of its statehood. . . . We have therefore, to this day, not ceased being a people, a spiritual nation, to which individuals belong in the dimension of spirit and thought and not in material terms. In practical reality every Jew is a citizen of the land in which he dwells, and it is his duty to be a good citizen, who accepts all the obligations of citizenship like all other nationals of the country.[34]

After 1881 Smolenskin walked no such tightrope. Now he explicitly urged "a policy of reducing the number of Jews in the countries where they are hated." This was to be achieved by a deliberate policy of encouraging emigration to Palestine by "substantial segments of the Jewish communities." [35]

Smolenskin, who grew into a vigorous opponent of Westernized "enlightenment" and of the Reform movement, saw no use in addressing his appeal for total emigration to those who "mocked and derided the whole heritage of Israel." At the other extreme,

It is also useless to argue with those who wait for a day of miraculous Redemption and who are afraid to approach the Holy Land until that day, lest they appear to be blasphemous. . . . We will address ourselves to the sensible people who do not belong to either of these extremes—to those who feel for their brethren and are willing to make sacrifices on the altar of love for their people. Such people will listen, understand, act, and succeed. We shall tell them that there is no other land that will lovingly accept the exiles save the Land of Israel, and that only there can they find truth and lasting peace.[36]

In the eyes of the sensible people, the potentialities of Israel for making a living would be a consideration. Smolenskin, accordingly, wrote of its economic potential in terms of commerce and manufacturing, as well as agriculture, which, as we have seen, was the sentimental favorite.

Another of the Eastern European Jews who anticipates the actual birth of modern Zionism was Leo Pinsker (1821–91). To an even greater degree than Smolenskin, Pinsker had committed himself to the integration of the Jews into Russian life. His father was one of the "enlightened" Jews of his time; Pinsker had, therefore, a modern Russian education and had trained as a physician. After the Crimean War he was decorated by the tsar for his medical services to the Russian army. This made him an even more ardent advocate of the Russification of the Jews. From the foundation in 1863 of the Society for the Spread of Culture among the Jews of Russia, Pinsker was one of its active members. Even the pogroms of 1871 did not shake his belief that assimilation to Russian culture was the most desirable course for the Jews to follow. The pogroms of 1881, however, both because of their widespread occurrence and because the frenzied mobs were triggered by members of the upper classes, the literati, and even the government, shook his belief in Russification. He resigned from the Society for the Spread of Culture among the Jews of Russia, and sought an alternative solution for the Jewish problem.

In 1882 Pinsker published a pamphlet called *Auto-Emanzipation: Mahnruf an seine Stammesgenossen von einem russischen Juden* (Self-emancipation: An appeal to his people by a Russian Jew). The Orthodox objected to Pinsker's position because it was not built on a religious foundation. His former associates in the cause of assimilation protested, both in Russia and abroad, Pinsker's treason to faith in humanity. Nevertheless Pinsker received a hearing and his ideas found followers—with a difference: since Pinsker himself was sufficiently removed from his religious background, he did not argue that the self-emancipation of the Jews had, necessarily, to establish a homeland in Palestine. At best, he considered Palestine preferable; but he was prepared to consider any tract of land, anywhere in the world, where a Jewish nation could exist in independence. His followers, however, were less secularized, and they insisted on moving with Pinsker's ideas toward an independent Jewish state in Palestine. Thus the proto-Zionist organization that developed out of Pinsker's pamphlet was the Love of Zion (*Hibbat Zion*) movement.[37]

*Hibbat Zion* gained adherents throughout Europe and even in the United States but was far less successful in achieving an adequate financial base. The movement aided in the establishment of a number of agricultural colonies in Palestine and, because of the interest of Baron Edmond de Rothschild, was able to support hospitals, schools, and other necessary institutions. The paternalism of Rothschild, however, precluded the emergence of a true spirit of independence, so that the colonies set up under *Hibbat Zion* auspices marked only a slight advance over the pattern of religious mendicancy that had prevailed for centuries. The Jews of Palestine, in somewhat larger numbers than in earlier times, still required constant benefactions from the Jews of the European and American world in order to maintain even the semblance of self-emancipation.[38]

## THE BIRTH OF MODERN ZIONISM

While the nationalist movement among the Jews made such small progress, the antagonist force of anti-Semitism spread rapidly in Europe. The increase of anti-Semitism had several roots. One was certainly that in an era of revolutionary zeal, especially on the part of the working classes, the Jews were a readily available scapegoat; the very visibility of the Jews in commerce lent plausibility to the sly hints of government-inspired publicists that the Jews were the real source of the miseries of the workers. Another was that, as the humanistic dreams of the eighteenth-century Enlightenment confronted the shock of the French Revolution, European culture experienced a "failure of nerve" and retreated from universalism to nationalism, from democracy to autocracy, from visions of the future to glorifications of the past. Theories of nationalism became increasingly romantic as the nineteenth century moved on. It is but a step from Hegel's declaration that "the state is the idea of Spirit in the external manifestation of human will and its freedom" [39] to Heinrich von Treitschke's assertion that "the evolution of the State is, broadly speaking, nothing but the necessary outward form which the inner life of a people bestows upon itself." [40] Yet that short step is the difference between a theory of nationalism still rooted in Reason and one grounded in a mystical worship of the state. In multinational Austria, where common language and common ethnic origin could not be made basic to the idea of nationality, Karl Renner and others proposed that a nationality is a community of destiny and culture (*Schicksals- und Kulturgemeinschaft*).[41] In France Ernest Renan described nationality as a plebiscite repeated daily, and Numa Denis Fustel de Coulanges declared, "True patriotism is not love of the soil, but love of the past, reverence for the generations which have preceded us," [42] a concept which Maurice Barrès developed into his "integral nationalism," the idea that each individual identifies his own spirit with the national past: "We are the product of a collective being which speaks in us. Let the influence of the ancestors be enduring and the sons will be vigorous and upright, and the nation one." [43] According to such theories the Jews could not be absorbed into a nation because they were not part of the national past.

In 1894 Captain Alfred Dreyfus of the French General

Staff was accused of being a traitor and a German spy. He was convicted by the conservative court in an obvious judicial plot, the purpose of which was to shake public confidence in the Third Republic. Barrès was one of the outstanding spokesmen for the anti-Dreyfusards and "the honor of the army." [44] Attending the trial, reporting on it and on its effects on French life, was a young Hungarian-Jewish journalist and literary dilettante, serving then as resident Paris correspondent of the Vienna *Neue Freie Presse*. Theodor Herzl (1860–1904), although he had met some anti-Semitism in his University days, was an almost completely "Westernized" Jew. His first real confrontation with the new anti-Semitism had been in France two years before the Dreyfus trial. As a result the Jewish problem became of major concern to him, though his reflections still did not lead him to break with his belief in the possibility of better understanding between Jew and Gentile. But the Dreyfus trial itself and the reactions of the French masses to it convinced him that the "ancient hatreds" could not be so readily subdued.

By June of 1895 Herzl had set forth in outline his theory of a Jewish national state; soon thereafter he penned an expanded form of his plan, addressed to the Rothschild family, whom he hoped to interest in his proposals. This pamphlet, in still further revised and expanded form, was published early in 1896 under the title *Der Judenstaat* (The Jewish state). From its publication we may date the birth of modern Zionism. Herzl's program is entirely secular; there seems to be no vestige in his thought of the older, religious idea of restoration. He writes as a modern secular nationalist proposing the establishment of yet another secular state. His explanation of the causes of anti-Semitism refers only in glancing fashion to religious intolerance; his chief stress falls on economic and political causes and shows his understanding of the relationship of anti-Semitism and emancipation:

Modern anti-Semitism is not to be confused with the persecution of the Jews in former times, though it does still have a religious aspect in some countries. The main current of Jew-hatred is today a different one. In the principal centers of anti-Semitism, it is an outgrowth of the emancipation of the Jews. When civilized nations awoke to the inhumanity of discriminatory legislation and enfranchised us, our enfranchisement came too late. Legislation alone no longer sufficed to emancipate us in our old homes. For in the ghetto we had remarkably developed into a bourgeois people and we emerged from the ghetto a prodigious rival to the middle class. Thus we found ourselves thrust, upon emancipation, into this bourgeois circle, where we have a double pressure to sustain, from within and from without. The Christian bourgeoisie would indeed not be loath to cast us as a peace offering to socialism, little though that would avail them.[45]

Herzl was completely unsentimental in his rejection of the pipe dream of transforming the Jews into agriculturalists in Europe, and thus, by diversifying the forms of Jewish participation in economic life, destroying the prejudice against them. He saw this plan as a residue of the eighteenth-century physiocratic school of economic doctrine, with its conception that agriculture is the only truly productive activity. In the first place, he said, the peasant is obsolescent: "His plow is unchanged; he sows his seed from the apron, mows with the time-honored scythe, and threshes with the flail. But we know that all this can now be done by machinery. . . . The peasant is, consequently, a type which is on the way to extinction." Moreover, those few regions in Europe where special conditions have led "desperate Jews" to adopt the peasant's mode of life "are the very hotbeds of anti-Semitism." [46]

Unsentimental, too, is Herzl's recognition that the solidarity of the Jews is itself one of the by-products of anti-Semitism.

Perhaps we *could* succeed in vanishing without a trace into the surrounding peoples if they would let us be for just two generations. But they will not let us be. After brief periods of toleration, their hostility erupts again and again. When we prosper, it seems to be unbearably irritating, for the world has for many centuries been accustomed to regarding us as the most degraded of the poor. Thus out of ignorance or illwill they have failed to observe that prosperity weakens us as Jews and wipes away our differences. Only pressure drives us back to our own; only hostility stamps us ever again as strangers. . . . We are one people—our enemies have made us one whether we will or not.[47]

Herzl did not see the common link of the Jewish people as religion or language, land or "blood." It is, he insisted, affliction that establishes the cohesiveness of the Jewish people.

His plan was realistic. It called for the setting up of two agencies, one policy making, to be called the Society of Jews, the other executive and administrative, to be called the Jewish Company. With the cooperation of these two agencies, a gradual migration of Jews to the chosen land—Herzl mentioned Argentina and Palestine as possibilities in *The Jewish State,* and later considered seriously a British proposal to establish the new state in Uganda—over a period of decades would be encouraged. Everything done by these settlers should be done by the most modern of methods. "It is silly to revert to older levels of civilization, as many Zionists propose." The first group should be those standing at the bottom of the economic scale:

The poorest will go first and cultivate the soil. They will construct roads, bridges, railways, and telegraph installations, regulate rivers, and provide themselves with homesteads, all according to predetermined plans. Their labor will create trade, trade will create markets, and markets will attract new settlers—for every man will go voluntarily, at his own expense and his own risk. The labor invested in the soil will enhance its value. The Jews will soon perceive that a new and permanent frontier has been opened up for that spirit of enterprise which has heretofore brought them only hatred and obloquy.[48]

In 1897, under Herzl's leadership, the First Zionist Congress convened at Basel to take steps toward the implementation of some version of Herzl's plan. More than two hundred delegates, from all over the world, were in attendance. Herzl himself addressed the Congress, as did his disciple, Max Nordau (1849–1923). Other speakers presented factual reports on the conditions of the Jews in various countries, explorations of various facets of Zionism, even proposals for the establishment of a Jewish University. The Congress led to the foundation of the Zionist Organization on a continuing basis, and to the formulation of a Zionist Program.[49]

Immediately after the Basel Congress, when he returned to Vienna, Herzl wrote in his diary, "At Basle I founded the Jewish State. If I were to say this today, I would be met by universal laughter. In five years, perhaps, and certainly in fifty, every one will see it." [50] That the sublime self-confidence of this statement was justified by the course of history should not blind us to the fact that it is the utterance of a man convinced of his own mission, of a Messianic leader. His Messianism was, however, not that of the traditional religious view. It was, rather, a Messianism in tune with the mystique of the later nineteenth-century varieties of nationalism, as can readily be seen from the sentence that followed the diary entry just quoted: "The State is already founded, in essence, in the will of the people of the State." [51] Whatever practical steps might be undertaken, whatever negotiations Herzl might enter into with ruling monarchs, whatever rational arguments he might advance in justification of his cause, his very insistence on the historical necessity of success because of the "will of the people" is conclusive evidence of his essential kinship with the romantic nationalism of his time.

Thus when Max Nordau, in 1902, affirmed that political Zionism differs from the religiously Messianic type of Zionism that had prevailed in an earlier time "in that it disavows all mysticism, no longer identifies itself with messianism, and does not expect the return to Palestine to be brought about by a miracle," he was overlooking the mystical and Messianic possibilities in politics—a mistake that we, in the latter half of the twentieth century, are less likely to make. After a brief nod in the direction of forces making for the new Zionism "in the inner impulses of Judaism itself," Nordau pointed out: "For the rest, Zionism is the result of two impulses which came from without: first, the principle of nationality, which dominated thought and sentiment in Europe for half a century and determined the politics of the world; second, anti-Semitism, from which the Jews of all countries suffer to some degree." [52] His analysis follows that of Herzl in emphasizing these two secular and practical forces at work in the world of his time, but fails to recognize the extent to which his own discipleship, as well as that of thousands of other Jews throughout the world, was testimony to the charismatic quality of Herzl's nonreligious Messianism.

### ZIONISM AS A RELIGION

It is neither possible nor proper in this context to detail all the debates over principle and the squabbles over the internal politics of the Zionist Organization in the two or three decades after the birth of the movement. Zionism was never a completely unified movement except in respect to the desire to set up a national homeland for the Jews. What steps should be taken to achieve that goal, how that homeland should be administered, who should lead the movement, where did Judaism and Jewish culture fit into the Zionist framework, and when the appropriate time for any action had come were all subjects of constant and often acrimonious discussion. Eastern European, Western European, and American Zionists differed on these questions. Bourgeois democratic Jews and Marxist socialist Jews argued the nature of Zionism incessantly. Assimilated Jews and traditionalists were in perpetual disagreement. Despite all this controversy, Zionism captured the imagination of the Jewish masses. It became, for the twentieth century, the vital issue in Jewish life.

This was the case even before 1917 brought increased hope by the promulgation of the Balfour Declaration:

His Majesty's Government view with favour the establishment in
Palestine of a national home for the Jewish people, and will use
their best endeavours to facilitate the achievement of this object,
it being clearly understood that nothing shall be done which may
prejudice the civil and religious rights of existing non-Jewish
communities in Palestine, or the rights and political status en-
joyed by Jews in any other country.[53]

Many factors in the British situation at the time led to this
pronouncement, notably the desire to mobilize Jewish sentiment in other countries in favor of the Allies. Whatever the
causes, the effect on the Jews was electric. Balfour's diplo-
matically turned phrases were read in synagogues all over the
world and discussed by preachers, teachers, and editors. It
was as if the long-awaited Restoration had already taken place
and the prophecies of the Bible had come true. Thousands of
Jews who had held back from Zionist affiliation now hastened
to join the movement and to add their strength for the re-
building of Zion, under the British mandate, after the end
of the First World War. The increase in the number of adherents to Zionism was paralleled by an increase in the number of factions within the Zionist movement.

The advent of Hitler's National Socialist government in
Germany in the 1930s, with its resurgent anti-Semitism and
its echoes in many other countries, provided a second major
stimulus to the Zionist movement. Under the spur of Hitler-
ism, confirmed opponents of the idea of a national homeland,
or even a Jewish nationality, were forced to face the need
for a land of refuge. Herzlian Zionism had combined both
elements, nationality and refuge from anti-Semitism. The
Balfour Declaration brought recruits into the Zionist fold by
heightening the optimistic hope of national independence
and achievement; Nazi anti-Semitic atrocities created Zionists by heightening the pessimistic sense that hatred of the
Jews and use of them as a scapegoat was a perennially recur-
ring feature of European life. Indeed, the fear of anti-Semitic
outbursts became so intense that Abba Hillel Silver (1893–

1963), an American Reform rabbi and Zionist leader, declared, in 1944:

The New World, for a time, made possible a pleasant sense of almost complete identification. That is no longer the case and in all probability will never be again. The Old World brand of anti-Semitism is here to stay. . . . America is not likely to go fascist, but fascistically-minded Americans, who will always be anti-Semites, will persist in large numbers. . . . What I am trying to say is that our lives as American Jews have now fallen into the pattern of Israel's millennial experience in Diaspora. . . . American Jews also have come to share, however reluctantly, the common and inescapable destiny of their fellow Jews in the rest of the world.[54]

The Balfour Declaration held out hope for the Jews in Palestine; Hitler and his forces made it seem clear that there was no hope for the Jews elsewhere.

The growth of Zionism in this period is to be attributed, not only to these external spurs, but also, in part, to its offering every individual something concrete that he could do as a personal contribution to the cause. Nothing is more frustrating than to be forced to sit idly by while great events are taking place on the stage of history—millions of one's fellows exterminated like vermin, and a new nation being brought to birth out of the ashes of history. Zionism, through its multiple agencies, made it unnecessary, almost impossible, for any Jew to sit by, to hold aloof and do nothing. This was, characteristically, especially true in America, perhaps because the American Jew has so often a feeling of guilt at being better off than his counterparts in other lands. For a time the Zionist wave in America had about it a revivalistic quality. It became a form of hysterical identification with the persecuted Jews of Central Europe. Social pressure operated to make Zionists as it had never operated in America to make adherents to any interpretation of Jewish tradition. Zionism became the national religion of the Jews of America.

Although Reform, Conservative, and Orthodox groups

went through similar stages in the acceptance of the Zionist cause, they passed through these stages at different rates of speed. Zionists were, at first, a small party within each group. The great bulk of each group was either indifferent or opposed to Jewish nationalism. Within the Conservative Movement the shift to a Zionist majority came most rapidly and with least disruption. For a time some difficulty was felt about the problem of dual allegiance, to America and to Zion, but the Zionist emphasis, within the Conservative Movement, tended to be more cultural than political, so it was relatively easy to show that the two forms of nationalism were not in conflict. Once this resolution had been achieved, Conservative Jews had little trouble accepting Zionism, especially since the Conservative orientation was so largely directed toward the Jewish community.[55] In both the Reform and the Orthodox groups the difficulty was a more complicated one and far less easy to resolve.

Reform Judaism had deliberately eliminated from its thought the conception of the Jews as a nation. "We have warmly, and earnestly enough, held that the Jews are not a nation. In accordance with this view, we have allowed the purely national holidays of Judaism to drop into the background and have expurgated the prayers for return to Jerusalem from the ritual of others." [56] Despite this elimination of the idea of Jewish nationhood, explicitly set forth in the Pittsburgh Platform, many of the older generation of Reform rabbis, including Gustave Gottheil of Temple Emanuel in New York and Bernard Felsenthal of Chicago, as well as younger men like Stephen S. Wise, had early found a vivifying faith in Zionism. For many years each annual meeting of the Central Conference of American Rabbis was confronted by a determined group of Zionist sympathizers trying to put on the record a more favorable resolution, but it was not until 1943 that the Central Conference finally passed the resolution asserting the compatibility of Zionism and Reform Judaism. The Reform lay organization, the Union of

American Hebrew Congregation had already, in 1937, in a carefully phrased resolution, affirmed "the obligation of all Jewry to aid [in building Palestine] as a Jewish homeland by endeavoring to make it not only a haven or refuge for the oppressed but also a center of Jewish culture and spiritual life." While these actions removed the official agencies of Reform Judaism from the anti-Zionist camp, it has been left to each congregation to determine what its positive stand shall be, and there are still two factions in Reform Judaism.[57]

Orthodox Judaism was also split, in a different fashion, between those who were prepared to accept a "political" return in lieu of a "miraculous" restoration (the Mizrachi organization) and others who were unwilling to give up the traditional supernatural Messianism (the Agudat Israel movement). The official Orthodox rabbinical council endorsed both movements. The split has not healed, but, as the younger generation of Orthodox laity matured, its support went overwhelmingly to the Mizrachi movement, leaving Agudat Israel with but a scanty following in the United States.[58] It should be noted, too, that as an Orthodox group the Mizrachi organization has maintained its separateness; it will cooperate but not affiliate with the Zionist Organization of America.

As recently as 1948 the strength of the Zionist Movement, forged out of such disparate elements, held together. To the shocked horror of some segments of American Jewry—chiefly at the two extremes of intransigent Reform and unyielding Orthodoxy—some rabbis went so far as to devote their sermons on the holiest of occasions to promoting support for Zionist activities or to making appeals for funds to be used in the upbuilding of the Jewish National Home. Whatever the formal religion of the Jews may have been, for a time it was support of Zion and Zionism that was their living faith. So intense was the devotion of American Jews to Zionism that in 1948, when the partition plan for Palestine was a major issue in the politics of the day, virtually the entire

Jewish population of the United States was turned into a pressure group for the achievement of Zionist objectives. The Synagogue Council of America, an organization representing both rabbinical and lay groups in Orthodox, Conservative, and Reform camps, called for a day of prayer, April 8, 1948, "to give expression to the shocked conscience of America at the inexplicable action of our Administration in reversing its Palestine policy" by abandoning the partition plan, and "to demand the fulfillment of the plighted word of this country and of the nations of the world, and to pray for God's help." [59]

The force of Zionism as a vital unifying factor in American Jewish life did not last beyond the achievement of the full independence of the State of Israel. While it continued, completely "secular" Jews, of the Labor Zionist wing of the movement, were able to work side by side with Mizrachi Orthodox Zionists, subordinating their many differences of opinion to the discipline of a common hope and a common goal. Community of Jewish experience, which in earlier days in America was sought, and only rarely found, in the unity of synagogal life, was, in the heyday of American Zionism, found in the struggle for realization of Jewish nationhood. Suddenly, however, to the surprise of observers and the dismay of Zionist leaders, the driving force of the ideal of nationhood no longer operated with as much power on the minds of American Jews. Organizations on whose active sympathy Zionist leaders had relied were no longer to be counted upon. Individuals dropped out of Zionist activities, and collections for Zionist purposes declined considerably, though the sale of State of Israel bonds has taken up much of the slack. Perhaps one reason for this is to be found in what has been called the "privatization" of American life; if so, it is another example of my thesis that Jewish attitudes are responsive to the attitudes prevalent in the communities among which the Jews live. Another possible reason is that many who were eager to help in establishing the independence of Israel felt that independence should mean readiness to continue without help. Whatever the reasons for this change of heart, it is sufficient here to record the fact that from the 1920s and 1930s to about 1950, there was a vital Jewish community in America, founded not in traditional religious faith but in Zionist hope transformed into a national religion. This was the nearest that the American Jewish community has ever come to complete unity. What will replace Zionism as a focus of unification—indeed, whether another such focus will ever arise—only the future can reveal.

# 6

*Was Emancipation a Mistake?*
*Mid-Twentieth-Century Appraisals*

The emancipation of the Jews of Western Europe came about as a by-product of the eighteenth-century age of Reason and Enlightenment, although the roots of emancipation go back to the middle ages and its completion was largely a phenomenon of the nineteenth century. Emancipation triggered a major crisis in the history of Judaism. The new status of the Jews in society compelled them to reexamine, from its perspective, their religious beliefs and practices, and to adjust their ways of living and of regarding life to those of the surrounding culture. The first response of many of the Jews of Western Europe was to welcome emancipation and its fruits and to reformulate the Jewish tradition, with varying degrees of innovation, so as to permit and even encourage the integration of individual Jews into the life of the modern Western nations. All the modern varieties of Judaism reveal, to a greater or lesser degree, the influence of emancipation and of the full entry of the Jews into the secular life of their communities. This influence is shown at its clearest in American Judaism, because the United States of America had few, if any, residues of a pre-emancipation outlook to overcome. Consequently American Judaism has been productive of the greatest number of interpretations of what it means to be a Jew under modern conditions and of the widest variety in these interpretations.

There can be no doubt that emancipated status has worked to the tremendous advantage of a vast number of individual Jews. They have had a fair field for the development and exploitation of their talents and have contributed to virtually every field of contemporary endeavor. But the very possibility of the entry of individual Jews into every aspect of life in modern societies has weakened the powers of the Jewish communal groupings. One reason for this is that a great many of the most capable Jews became leaders of the general community and had little—in some cases, no—time or attention to spare for the Jewish community. Their works and their words became part of the broad stream of Western culture, but they spoke and acted not as Jews but as Western men. Some of these leaders became so dedicated to the cause of humanity in general that they no longer identified themselves as Jews; others retained a slight sense of identification but participated in Jewish life to so small a degree that they added little strength to it. A second reason for the sapping of the strength of the Jewish communities, in the long run perhaps more important than the loss of leadership potential, is that when the Jewish community no longer was the only possible buffer to stand between the Jews and the general government, when, indeed, the Jews as citizens needed no intermediary between them and their government, the sanctions of the community in other respects rapidly disappeared. In the past, when one had either remained a faithful member of the Jewish community or stood completely outside of organized society, the threat of communal ban, or excommunication, had real force. Once there were options beside conversion to Christianity, excommunication became an empty gesture, more valuable in assuaging the hurt feelings of the excommunicators than in compelling the conformity of the recalcitrant member. Because the Jewish community no longer retained the function that had given it its coercive power, whatever the Jews as individuals may have gained by emancipation, the Jews as a group unquestionably lost.

Furthermore, by the time that emancipation had advanced far enough for patterns of interpretation of Judaism based upon emancipation to have been developed, the European world and, to a far lesser extent, the American world had retreated from the rationality of the Enlightenment out of which the idea of emancipation had been born to a new irrationalism. Nationalisms of an increasing degree of romantic emphasis upon continuity of blood, attachment to soil, and reverence for tradition replaced the universality of the age of reason, and in these theories of nationalism it was as hard to find a place for the Jews as it had been for the medieval mind to find a place for them in its society. At the other extreme of social thought, the multiple forms of socialism which preserved the internationalism of the Enlightenment and made little of national boundaries insisted upon the impassability of class barriers and the inevitability of class warfare. The socialist mystique asserted the community of workers of the world across religious and ethnic lines as well as across national boundaries. Adherence to socialism meant, then, a weakening of the sense of solidarity with all other Jews, regardless of class. Thus, at the very time that alternative patterns for emancipated Jewry were being elaborated, they were already partly irrelevant to newer conditions.

Under these circumstances, it is small wonder that the fruits of emancipation turned bitter in the mouths of many Jews. Some, because the traditional rabbinical form of Judaism seemed to them a force that could hold the Jews together despite all the disintegrating features of the modern world, tried to live, as far as possible, as if the modern world did not exist. Whatever success such enclaves had for their first members, their permanence could not be assured, because it is not possible to reject a part only of one's world. Over any length of time one cannot simultaneously accept sixteenth-century morality and nineteenth-century technology. Even in an enclave, however, one cannot live in the nineteenth-century world without accepting nineteenth-century technology. Others turned completely to the world, rejecting the Judaism in which they had been nurtured and substituting the pseudo religion of socialism, often justifying themselves to themselves by arguing that in socialism the universalistic prophetic social morality of Judaism was preserved without the taint of superstition. Still others became Jewish nationalists, working for the establishment of a secular Jewish state, preferably in Palestine, but elsewhere if circumstances so dictated.

It took some time, as we have seen, for the residues of earlier Jewish ideas of miraculous, Messianic restoration to be completely eliminated from Jewish nationalism. By the end of the nineteenth century, however, a thoroughly secularized Jew, Theodor Herzl, bred entirely in Western modes of thought, created modern political Zionism as a reaction to the new anti-Semitism that burgeoned in the wake of the newer European theories of nationalism. Herzl and his followers, some of them even more sharply than Herzl himself, argued that the Jews needed a state of their own, a national government of their own, an army and a diplomatic corps of their own, to protect them against their non-Jewish fellow citizens in the very same Western nations that had given birth to emancipation a century earlier. This is, surely, a very clear indication of the direction and the distance that Western Europe had traveled between the end of the eighteenth century and the end of the nineteenth century. Later events in Russia, in Poland, and preeminently in Germany were to confirm Herzl's analysis of the new situation and to lead not only to a Zionist mass movement, in many respects the most dynamic aspect of twentieth-century Jewish life, but also to the turning inward of Jewish life upon itself, the attempt in the lands of emancipated strangerhood to restore a significant Jewish community, a revived attention to Jewish culture and its history, and the reassertion, in many forms, of theories of Jewish particularism.

Moreover, the philosophic sources drawn upon by newer Jewish thinkers in constructing the theoretical groundwork for their postemancipation attitudes are themselves part and parcel of the irrationalism of the later nineteenth and the twentieth centuries. In the earlier period Jewish thinkers developed their versions of modern Judaism in terms derived chiefly from the rationalistic philosophies of nineteenth-century Germany. Later Jewish thinkers follow the philosophies of irrationalism that prevail in the twentieth-century world. Some accept as the basis of their thought one or another type of Life-philosophy (*Lebensphilosophie*)—pragmatism, vitalism, or historicism—which in all its forms emphasizes connectedness and evolutionary development, and therefore readily serves as a foundation for a renewed emphasis on the values of tradition. Others take their departure from Existentialism, the latest form of subjectivity, which emphasizes the disjunction of individual and society, stresses personal response as the central element in religion, and minimizes the importance of the group to religion. Neither Life-philosophy nor Existentialism appears in its most extreme form among Jewish thinkers, but both of these divergent nonrational philosophies are present in twentieth-century Jewish thought.

The rationalistic, emancipated philosophy of Judaism that prevailed in the nineteenth century assumed that it was possible to be simultaneously true to both Judaism and one of the Western nations, as Isaac M. Wise put it, to live "as Jews in the synagogue, and Americans everywhere else." [1] Once Messianic nationalism had been eliminated and the idea of a Jewish mission among the nations substituted for it, the Jews' homeland was wherever they lived. Later thinkers,

under the influence of newer theories of nationalism, regarded nationhood differently. For them it became one of
the fixed poles of Jewish thought. The acceptance of nationhood in this fashion led them to a reaffirmation of the opposite pole, that of strangerhood or alienation. The antithesis
of nationhood and strangerhood, Homeland and Exile, could
not have been accepted by any of the major Jewish thinkers
of the earlier time. It would have been as unsavory to Samson Raphael Hirsch as to Abraham Geiger, despite the Hegelian legacies in the thought of both. Yet the assertion of this
antithesis has become a commonplace to their successors.

Yitzhak F. Baer, for example, centers his important little
book called simply *Galut* (Exile) on this polar opposition. If
once we grant, he says, the fact of Jewish nationhood, then it
follows that there is a Homeland, a spot on the face of the
earth where the Jews of the world properly belong, a place
they rightly call home. Anywhere else in the world the Jews
are exiles, perpetual strangers, aliens in a foreign land. Because of their strangerhood, they are unable to fulfil their
destinies as Jews. The meaning of Jewish life is to be sought
in the tensions of the dialectical antithesis of Homeland and
Exile.[2] Ludwig Lewisohn, whose earlier writings spoke for
an assimilationist attitude, was convinced, toward the end of
his life, of the validity of an irreconcilable antithesis of Exile
and Homeland. On the basis of this conviction he argued
that, even in America, a Jew could be only a partially realized
person.[3] This position points up the excellent distinction
made by Arthur A. Cohen between the concept of Dispersion
(Diaspora) and that of Exile. Dispersion, Cohen notes, is a
fact of history; the Jewish people have been, for many centuries, dispersed and scattered among the nations of the earth.
Exile refers to the same phenomenon, but is not merely a
description of the fact; it is an interpretation, a cosmic evaluation, of that fact.

The Dispersion is but the historical fact. The Exile transposes
that fact into a different order of apprehension, and a construct

of faith emerges. . . . The Exile is a cosmic, not an historical, event in Jewish tradition. . . . The historical catastrophe is elevated to a metahistorical reality . . . [the] dialectic of expectation and despair, conservation and perpetuation, unfolded many times in the two-thousand-year Exile of the Jew. It was the Exile, however, which cadenced the rhythm of Jewish existence, elevating it to expectation and bringing it low to the funereal despair of renewed waiting.[4]

Cohen, however, makes clear that in his thought the transhistorical idea of Exile loses force as Jewish life moves closer to actual events. When the Jew was shut up in the ghetto, he could maintain the distance from history necessary to interpret it "with a supernatural eye." [5] Once emancipation had broken down the ghetto walls, one could talk of Dispersion, but no longer of Exile. With the founding of the State of Israel, the Dispersion, the "physical incubus of Diaspora," is over. "The question still remains . . . : Is the Exile ended?"[6] And this religious question Cohen answers in the negative; the Exile is a universal principle and signifies man's alienation from God.

Another interesting reading of the polar antagonism of Exile and Homeland is to be found in the thought of Eliezer Berkovits, an able representative of Orthodox Judaism. The general tone of his thought has similarities to that of Samson Raphael Hirsch; the chief differences are to be found in Berkovits' special version of Jewish nationalism. In this view Berkovits is far removed from the position of the secular Zionists. Zionism, as it has developed in the State of Israel, meets with condemnation because it "does not of itself mean religious and cultural regeneration, nor does it automatically bring about the healing of the breach between Torah and life. On the contrary, its reappearance may emphasize the breach by revealing the contrast between the new form of life and the world of an ancient tradition." [7] Berkovits is dedicated to that ancient tradition in its historic development. To it he would gladly sacrifice all that the Jews have gained in the past centuries of secular participation. While, he admits, the modern Israeli in modern Israel is "a new youth in which any nation might take pride," the very fact that this modern Israeli is creating a secular state leads Berkovits to criticize him for being only doubtfully a Jew. Zionism is not acceptable to Berkovits, then, because "the new Jewish reality in Palestine is, for the time being, overwhelmingly of a nature that cannot be reconciled with the aims and intentions of historic Judaism." [8]

If a secular interpretation of the Homeland is unacceptable, so too is the tolerance of a secular emancipated status. Berkovits criticized Samson Raphael Hirsch for having made too great a concession to emancipation, to the neglect of the idea of Exile. In this idea Berkovits finds the central and inescapable theme, the everlasting meaning of Judaism. This is the perpetual strangerhood to which the Jews are destined:

We went into Galut to bide our time there, to wait; to wait, however long it might be, until the time when the establishment of the State of God on earth might be attempted once more. Galut is no break in the history of Judaism; it is an inevitable step on the way to the final realization. . . . We have often been trampled upon, but let us thank God that it was not we who trampled upon justice, decency, freedom, human dignity, whenever it suited our selfish purposes. Let us be grateful to the Galut; it has freed us from the guilt of national existence in a world in which national existence meant guilt.[9]

Berkovits reveals an attitude toward emancipation that we have not met before. It is an attitude fully as extreme as that of the early Reformers, though of an opposite nature. To Berkovits emancipation was altogether a mistake, a curse, not a blessing, because it led the Jews to renounce their special status as eternal strangers and to secularize their lives.

## RESURGENCE OF THE CULTURAL EMPHASIS

One of the earliest forms of criticism of the Zionist idea was that its form of nationalism was too completely divorced from Jewish culture, rather than from Jewish religion. Even before the formal organization of Zionism had taken place Eliezer Ben-Yehudah (1858–1923), while agreeing with Peretz Smolenskin that the Jews had to develop into a modern secular nation, insisted upon the need for a concurrent revival of the Hebrew language. From 1881 to the time of his death, in Palestine and in the United States he dedicated himself to the remaking of Hebrew from an ancient tongue into a medium of modern communication. It is important to stress the fact that Ben-Yehudah's concern was not in the least religious. It was simply his conviction that the revival of the Jewish nation and the revival of Hebrew were inseparably linked.[10]

Another of the early critics of Zionism from within was Asher Zvi Ginsberg (1856–1927), who wrote under the pen name of Ahad Ha-Am (One of the People). Ahad Ha-Am's belief was that national independence was not to be achieved by a mass movement of a purely political nature, but by the development of a modernized cultural and intellectual life. His conception of the culture to be aimed at was secular and literary. Only, thus, he thought, could the Jewish spirit be restored to vitality. He voiced this criticism and the conviction on which it was based in his first article, an examination of the small achievements of the Love of Zion (*Hibbat Zion*) movement, and he continued to present his views after Herzlian Zionism had come to the birth. His system of thought, called Cultural Zionism, has had particular appeal within Conservative Judaism.

Ahad Ha-Am used the term "Judaism" to mean the entire spiritual and intellectual life of the Jewish people, of which the Jewish religion was but one expression. Jewish religion and Jewish national spirit had a distinctive relation to each other in his thought, for, as he wrote to Rabbi Judah L. Magnes in 1910,

In my view our religion is national—that is to say, it is a product of our national spirit—but the reverse is not true. If it is impossible to be a Jew in the religious sense without acknowledging

our nationality, it is possible to be a Jew in the national sense
without accepting many things in which religion requires belief.[11]

He thought that his formulation of this relationship clarified
also the difference between the political Zionism of the emancipated but disappointed Jews of Western Europe, for whom
Jewish culture is "a closed book," and the Love of Zion of the
unemancipated Eastern European Jews, who are genuinely attached to the age-old Jewish culture.

The eastern form of the spiritual problem is absolutely different
from the western. In the West it is the problem of the Jews; in
the East, the *problem of Judaism*. The first weighs on the individual; the second, on the nation. The one is felt by Jews who
have had a European education; the other, by Jews whose education has been Jewish. The one is a product of anti-Semitism, and
is dependent on anti-Semitism for its existence; the other is a
natural product of a real link with a millennial culture, and it
will remain unsolved and unaffected even if the troubled of the
Jews all over the world attain comfortable economic positions,
are on the best possible terms with their neighbors, and are admitted to the fullest social and political equality.[12]

What then is the real problem of Judaism? It is that its older
traditional form is no longer adequate to modern life, but
that to abandon that form before a substitute has been produced by the national spirit of the Jews themselves will
destroy Jewish life. Yet "In exile, Judaism cannot . . . develop its individuality in its own way."[13]

Ahad Ha-Am's solution of this dilemma is to be found in
the return to Palestine and the natural emergence there of
a modern Jewish national culture. For this purpose it is not
necessary to create an independent state; a diversified Jewish
settlement is enough for the time being. A cultural center
is needed rather than a political center. What is important
is that, in its confrontation with modern culture, Judaism
should not be overwhelmed, as it inevitably must be under
conditions of exile. For "It is not only the Jews who have

come out of the ghetto; Judaism has come out, too . . . (or is coming out) of its own accord, wherever it has come into contact with modern culture." [14] When Judaism leaves the ghetto its essential being is endangered unless it has a congenial native soil in which to revitalize its cultural life.[15] It was from the disciples of Ahad Ha-Am, including the great Zionist leader Chaim Weizmann (1874–1952), the poet Hayyim Nahman Bialik (1873–1934), and the administrator Judah L. Magnes (1877–1948), that the impetus to found the Hebrew University in Jerusalem as one of the earliest creations of the Zionist administration drew its strength.

Ahad Ha-Am, through his secular studies, had gradually weaned himself away from the attachment to Jewish religion implanted in him by his early education. Franz Rosenzweig (1886–1929), the most thoroughgoing antirationalist among modern Jewish thinkers, had virtually no contact with religion of any sort during his formative years. His academic training was in philosophy; his family background was one of assimilation. By 1913 he was inclined to follow his friend, Eugen Rosenstock-Huessy, in converting to Christianity. He grew convinced, however, in the course of his discussions with Rosenstock-Huessy, that in order to become a Christian properly he should repeat in his own life the life experience of the founders of Christianity. They had been Jews at the time that they accepted the new message of Jesus; Rosenzweig decided that he should try to find himself religiously in the Jewish atmosphere of the synagogue and from that position attempt to break through to Christian religious conviction. What happened was that instead of breaking through to Christianity he discovered in his own life experience the meaning of Judaism. From this time to the end of his life, despite the limitations imposed upon him by service in World War I and, thereafter, by a creeping paralysis, he devoted himself to Jewish scholarship. He wrote, in the Existentialist vein, a remarkably penetrating philosophy of Judaism, called *Der Stern der Erlösung* (The star of redemption), published in 1921. In addition, Rosenzweig contributed greatly to the development of postwar Jewish education in Germany and strove to provide a platform on which other wholly emancipated German Jews like himself could find their way back to Judaism even as he had.

It was Rosenzweig's conviction that a philosophy had to be personal. He made no attempt to achieve the sort of impersonal standpoint, above the strains and stresses of life, that philosophers of the rationalistic schools have always sought. He did not wish to be what George Santayana called a "spectator of all time and all existence." Philosophy was neither about abstract problems nor about life in general, but about the concrete, individual life of the person doing the thinking. It was, therefore, himself that he wrote about. He had been brought up without any acquaintance with the customs of Jewish life in the ghetto, as a completely emancipated Western man. After his return to Judaism, when he looked for a foundation on which men like himself could erect a structure of "living Jewishness," [16] he was forced to conclude that the effects of emancipation had been tragic. Jewish life was unified before emancipation; its three elements—the home, the synagogue, and the law—were unseparated. Emancipation broke them into three separate fragments. Each had been transformed into a specialized unit in a secularized world.

Rosenzweig did not believe, however, that the unity of these elements could be restored in the external world unless and until the fragmentation within each individual's conception of himself had been made whole again. He conceived the emancipation to have destroyed the unity of the individual by breaking his affairs up into separate specialized segments. Partial Jewishness was the consequence, and partial Jewishness is inadequate; each must be able to say to himself "I am wholly Jewish."

And there is indeed no other way to become completely Jewish; the Jewish human being arises in no other way. All recipes, whether Zionist, orthodox, or liberal, produce caricatures of men, that become more ridiculous the more closely the recipes are followed. And a caricature of a man is also a caricature of a Jew; for as a Jew one cannot separate the one from the other. There is one recipe alone that can make a person Jewish and hence—because he is a Jew and destined to a Jewish life—a full human being: that recipe is to have no recipe.[17]

The road back to total Jewishness lies in total immersion in the study of Jewish culture, not by listening to lectures about Judaism or by stressing the observance of legal minutiae, but by participating in small study and discussion groups in which the classical documentary sources of Judaism are sifted energetically and sincerely to find their meaning as religious truths to guide present-day Jewish life. Modern secularism, based upon the dogma that this world is all that counts, is to be defeated not by turning away from the world but by bringing the culture of the Jewish people into vital relevance to the life of Jews in the world.

RESPONSES TO SECULARIZATION

Rosenzweig's early death meant that he had neither the opportunity for a full theoretical elaboration of his position nor the chance for the complete testing of his theories in life that he had anticipated. How fruitful his ideas might have been, how they might have changed after confrontation with the specter of Nazism, what differences might have been made by the successes of Zionism—these questions are forever unanswerable. At most we can speculate that his thought might have developed along the same lines as that of his friend and fellow worker, Martin Buber (1878–1965). Like Rosenzweig, Buber was a member of a Western European, emancipated family. His only contacts with traditional Judaism in his childhood came during visits to his grandfather, a distinguished Polish-Jewish scholar, living in an atmosphere in which the pietism of the Hassidic movement prevailed. In Buber's own home traditional rituals and home ceremonials were not observed, and he has remained without any nostalgic emotion for these cohesive bonds of Jewish group solidarity. His university studies led him to become a student of mysticism, especially in non-Jewish contexts. He also studied sociology of the metaphysical type that was prominent in German academic circles when he was a young man, the search for the inner bond that united the individual to all mankind in ideal community.

When Martin Buber became interested in gaining an understanding of Judaism, he worked through to a most intense supernaturalism. He found the distinctive note of all Jewish thought to be that God is ever-present in all of life. Accepting this as the core of his own position, Buber, the Western European, emancipated Jew, reacted against the specialization and compartmentalization of modern secular life by a renewed and revivified emphasis on the omnipresence of God. He reacted, too, against modern rational or scientific views that interpret God as a Force or a Power, insisting that God is the Person who binds all together in unity and community. All life is holy, hallowed by the presence of God. Here is another reason for Buber's lack of concern for ritual and ceremonial acts; they pale into insignificance beside the awe-inspiring realization that God can be seen in everything and can be reached by means of "every innocent act." [18] Buber's kinship with Existentialism is seen at its closest here. Each individual person must come into living and direct confrontation with God, by himself and not by any form of mediation. In the reflection of his meeting with God, man may also join with his fellows in the making of social institutions. Social cohesion without the sense of the ever-presence of God is merely aggregation; with this Presence, it becomes community.

Buber's view of the relation between man and God is irreducibly subjective. It is not derived from institutions, revealed scriptures, traditions, laws, or any other objectively identifiable and specifiable source. Each man must meet God

for himself and in his own life. Where Buber differs from
most other Existentialists is that, despite this extreme subjectivity, his position does not reach its climax with the isolated individual—even at the moment of meeting God. The
climax is later; it comes in the building of human community
with the realization of God's perpetual presence therein.
Originally, in the early years of the twentieth century, Buber
had been an active cultural Zionist, following the lead of
Ahad Ha-Am, seeing in Jewish nationalism not merely the
establishment of a state but also the re-creation of a Jewish
culture. Gradually, however, he came to reject the agnosti-
cism of Ahad Ha-Am and to believe that the distinctive note
of Jewish character—the Jewish soul—was to be found
neither in legalistic puritanism nor in ascetic purity but in
immanent spirituality, in the realization that the spirit of
God is present in all life. Nothing can be alien to Judaism in
which the spirit of God is present; therefore all life is holy.

When Buber had reached this point in the development of
his thought he was convinced that the mystical pietism of
the Hassidim exemplified both the sanctification of all life
and the essence of spiritual community. He valued particularly the fact that Hassidic piety involved a ready acceptance
of the immanence of God, concerning itself little with dogma
and ritual, but rather attempting to establish a human community on the foundation of the truth of divine presence. Of
all the elements of Hassidism that Buber stressed, the most
relevant to our understanding of his response to secularism
is his interpretation of the Hassidic Messianic view. Buber
claims that in Hassidic thought the Messianic redemption of
the world is to be prepared by men not in extraordinary acts,
not by asceticism or puritanism, but by the sanctification of
the "deeds of the everyday."

The intention of the divine revelation is to form men who can
work for the redemption of the world. By this is not meant one
single messianic act, but the deeds of the everyday, which prepare
for the messianic fulfillment. . . . He who does a mizwah [fulfils

a commandment] with complete kawanah [concentrated intention], that is completes an act in such a way that his whole existence is gathered in it and directed towards God, he works on the redemption of the world, on its conquest for God.[19]

This form of expression suggests that God needs man's help: but means not that God could not have redeemed the world without man's help, only that God "wills to have need of man." Specifically, God's will is that man should be of assistance in completing the work of creation, and since God wills this aid, "the use of man for this work becomes an effective reality."[20]

One cannot speak of man's part in the work or of God's part in the work, or, for that matter, of a collaboration between man and God. "God and man do not divide the government of the world between them; man's action is enclosed in God's action, but it is still real action." Each moment of every person's life is part of a continuous series of moments of creation and it is also part of a continuous series of moments of redemption. "It falls within creation in that it is made; it is tied and bound to redemption in virtue of its power for making."[21] Just as the work of creation is renewed by God every day, so man carries on the work of redemption every day. In terms such as these, every action done with a simple heart in complete turning toward God is Messianic action. The secular is sacralized when every act of man is viewed as a fulfillment of the task for which God needs man, the task of transforming the actual into the ideal.[22]

In sharp contrast to Buber's Existential way of transforming secular life into the vehicle of redemption stands the Reconstructionist philosophy of Mordecai M. Kaplan (1881–    ). Kaplan's Eastern European childhood was lived in an atmosphere of most observing, literalist orthodoxy, in which, as he has pointed out in an autobiographical narrative, he learned the minutiae of observance before he was involved in any formal schooling process.[23] In his college years, in the United States, Kaplan became engrossed in the study of the social sciences and was particularly impressed by Emile Durkheim's sociological theory of the function of religion as the repository of all that a culture holds sacred— the *sancta* of the culture, to use the technical term that Kaplan himself prefers. Through his study of Durkheim, Kaplan also derived the idea that the sense of unity and continuity that is produced by religion depends on what is done, rather than what is said, or on the interpretation that is placed upon what is done. It is, therefore, the interpretations, or, as Kaplan calls them in a recent work,[24] the "rationales," that can change in response to novel conditions without destroying the inner bond of a group, provided only that the things done, the observances, remain relatively constant.

This combination of respect for traditional behavior and dissatisfaction with the (equally traditional) theology of Judaism has provided the coloration of Kaplan's whole personal philosophy and that of the Reconstructionist movement of which he was the founder. Early in his maturity he formulated the principle of Reconstructionism: keep, as far as possible, observances intact, but assign to them new meanings in line with modern ideas. Over the course of the years he has found it necessary to stretch the principle by being more selective in regard to which observances are to be kept intact. Now he says that an "objective and adequate rationale for Judaism of our day . . . has to *select* from the Judaism of the past those beliefs and practices which, either in their original or in a reinterpreted form, are compatible with what we now recognize to be authentic." [25] What we now recognize as authentic must cohere with our other knowledge; it must not be a special compartment which we open only on those occasions conventionally called "religious," and keep tightly closed all the rest of the time.

Reconstructionism requires, then, that we recognize the qualities of the times in which we live and reinterpret Judaism so that it can serve us as a guide to living in the world.

"For the Jews," Kaplan said recently, "there can be no higher purpose than that of exemplifying the art of so living individually and collectively as to contribute to the intellectual, moral and spiritual progress of mankind." [26] For the follower of Kaplan, any attempt to construct an enclave of "pure" Jewishness without regard to the surrounding environment would be a retreat from the world. In the long run such a retreat is either self-defeating, because it falls into irrelevance, or defeated by the environment. If Jews are to contribute to the progress of mankind, it must be by advancing into the future, not by retreating into the past.

Kaplan's position requires the recognition that the Jewish people has been secularized and is living in a secular environment. It does no good to preach against secularization or to try to turn back the clock; history is irreversible. The only way to handle the secularization of life is to discover what meanings are holy in a secular world and then to celebrate these holy meanings in the old forms. Pour the new twentieth-century ideas into the age-old bottles of traditional observance. Without this conscious and deliberate introduction of new ideas the old practices will have no relevance to the lives of Jews—especially potential intellectual leaders among the Jews—and will either be discarded, along with any significant attachment to Judaism, or, if they are maintained, will be kept up in fossil form.

Traditionally, the three central themes of Jewish theology have been God, the Torah, and Israel. Kaplan has rethought each of these, in the light of his total position, akin to that of Emile Durkheim in sociology and John Dewey in philosophy. He has never merely advocated the rejection of any traditional position; in every case, he works out a suitable and, to his mind, more satisfactory alternative, which he then offers as a substitute. It must be remembered that Kaplan is unusually aware of modern currents of thought and unusually sensitive to them. What he regards as completely untenable in the light of modern knowledge may strike most people as completely tenable in the light of *their* knowledge. The recent agitation in England's United Synagogue, in which a rabbi and the congregation that supports him have been excluded from the community, in one of the most advanced nations of the world, for presuming to question the doctrine of literal inspiration of the Torah, indicates to how small a fraction of the world's Jews of today Kaplan's Reconstructionism is addressed.[27]

Kaplan has long abandoned the traditional idea of a personal God. He denies the possibility of miraculous interventions as inconsistent with a modern, scientific view of the uniformity of nature. God, for him, is a power other than ourselves in the universe that makes for the realization of our ideals, especially our ideals of righteousness. He does not understand this power to be supernatural; it is, to his mind, part of the natural order of the universe that there is such a power and that it should operate, even as the other powers in nature do, consistently and with absolute regularity.

His view of the second of the major elements of Jewish theology, the Torah, is again nonsupernatural. He does not conceive the Torah as divinely revealed, but rather as the record of the struggles of the Jewish people to educate its own conscience. The Torah, is, he says, "an expression of human nature at its best, the most articulate striving of man to achieve his salvation or self-fulfilment, and an expression of his most conscious recognition that only through righteousness can he achieve it." [28] Functionally, the Torah is a constant process of reinterpretation. "The integration of contemporary knowledge concerning the improvement of human nature and human society into the cultural and spiritual heritage of the Jewish people is the process of expanding the Torah, both in concept and in content." [29] What is needed today is an interpretation—Kaplan borrows Ahad Ha-Am's suggestion of *torah sh'belev* (Torah of the Educated Heart) —which will supply purpose and meaning to Jewish existence in the world of today, and "impel the Jewish People to make of itself a people in the image of God." [30]

It is with respect to the third concept, Israel, that Kaplan's thought is both most traditional and most radical, as well as very deeply indebted to Ahad Ha-Am. He breaks completely with the idea that Judaism is only a religion, comparable to other religions; he rejects the rationalistic and enlightened point of view that lies behind the Reform philosophy of Judaism. Judaism is, rather, the "advancing civilization of the Jewish People." [31] Thus Kaplan follows the French sociologists in seeing religion as primarily an affair of the group, rather than of individuals. The central reality of the Jewish tradition is neither God nor the Torah, but Israel, the Jewish People. The individuality of the individual Jew is a product of the group life of the Jewish People. There is an organic connection of the individual and the group. Kaplan claims that this has always been the meaning of Jewish religion. "Jewish religion has always assumed that, for man to maintain his God-likeness, he has to be the product of a people which orders its life in accordance with the will of God, or God-given Torah. That was the kind of people ancient Israel aspired to become." [32] This is expressed in terms of ancient concepts of revelation and of God; it requires translation into a modern mode of speech, thus: "Built into the Jewish consciousness is the striving to have the Jewish People foster a type of civilization that is calculated to render man fully and divinely human." [33]

Because, in his historic view, Judaism "is the only religion of mankind, which, from its very inception, has been based on the ongoing history of a people in its relation to mankind," [34] Kaplan attaches tremendous importance to the educational and cultural activities of the group as ways of promoting the integration of all Jews within the community and thus preserving the vitality of Jewish religion and renewing the spirit of Jewish worship. For these reasons, too, he has been a pioneer in the effort to reconstitute the Jewish community as a significant unit of Jewish life. He brings to this effort a conception of community which is essentially ethical and democratic. He is a keen student of democracy, which he interprets not merely as a political form but as a moral and religious way of life, a way of salvation. Democracy, he says, replaces the will to live by the will to live abundantly; he identifies the goal of abundant life as the naturalistic equivalent of the supernatural idea of salvation.

### THE JEWISH COMMUNITY

The stress placed on the idea of community by both Martin Buber and Mordecai Kaplan reinforces our earlier realization that the Jewish community was a major casualty of emancipation. Although the community did not go out of existence everywhere, it lost much of its force when it could no longer speak for all the Jews of any area and when it could no longer use social pressure to compel its own members to conformity. In the United States of America, where there has never been a community, the Jews of the twentieth century have apparently felt its absence as a serious deficiency. There has been some measure of success in America in federating Jewish agencies in the field of welfare activities, but, despite repeated attempts, a permanent national organization crossing all lines of internal division has never developed. There has been one major attempt in recent Jewish thought to set forth the conditions of community organization in full awareness of all the factors operating to prevent such organization. It is the social aspect of Kaplan's philosophy of Judaism, but it has gained the attention and support of many who do not accept the other aspects of Kaplan's thought.

The program rests on three basic principles which attempt to provide for centralized organization without abandoning democratic diversity. Kaplan's first principle takes care of theological differences by proposing that eligibility for mem-

bership shall be extended to all who desire to aid in fostering
Jewish life, however they may understand the form and content of Jewish life. Later expansions of the statement of this
principle make clear that Kaplan means to include here not
only those affiliated with Orthodox, Conservative, or Reform
synagogues, but also the unsynagogued, the "secular Jew."
The relative importance, for Kaplan, though not necessarily
for all who follow his general position, of different types of
organization within the pattern of the community is shown
in the second principle, assigning primacy to organizations
whose chief function is to heighten Jewish consciousness—
synagogues, cultural organizations, schools—over those whose
services to the development of Jewish consciousness are
secondary, like the welfare organizations of all sorts. Samuel
Dinin has pointed out that in the community councils that
have thus far been established, there has been widespread
failure to observe this second principle.[35] Kaplan's theories
of the nature of democracy lead to his third principle of
community organization: each group that is engaged in the
performance of a specific task shall continue what it is doing,
but shall also be represented in the deliberations of the community council. The intent of these three principles is that:

Every organized Jewish community will have a general membership, a democratically representative governing council that shall
determine its policies, an administrative committee and executive officers to supervise the execution of these policies, various
functional bureaus to direct the day-to-day activities of the community under the control of the council, and organizations for
specific Jewish purposes such as already exist.[36]

Within this inclusive organization the constituent groups
are to be entitled to full autonomy except for administration
of property and allocation of budget. Kaplan recognized that
granting this much self-determination might hamper the community program, but he considered this a lesser evil than
"unwise regimentation." For Kaplan, the vital point is that
these community councils should not be representative of

every Jew equally, in total disregard of the intensity and variety of his Jewish concerns, but should be representative of "every Jewish interest or tendency which is manifest in the community." [37]

One great problem that arises in considering this plan is the ambiguity of the role assigned to the synagogue as the primary agency of Jewish spiritual life. This may not be the problem for Kaplan himself and for his followers that it is for others, since he regards Judaism as a civilization and asserts that within that civilization the Jewish religion is essentially the heightened consciousness of the interests and values of the group. Because of this belief Kaplan has insisted on a revival of cultural nationalism, in which all aspects of Jewish experience and culture are integrated with the Jewish religion. With conscious paradox Kaplan has even held that it is in the best interest of Jewish religion to stress Jewish secular culture. "The spiritual regeneration of the Jewish people demands that religion cease to be its sole preoccupation." [38] But it is precisely at this point that many thoughtful and concerned Jews cannot accept a definition of the nature of Jewish community that seems to them to invert Jewish values by seeing communal life as the source of worship, instead of worship as the inspiration of communal life.

It would be well if the Jews of America could borrow from their Protestant neighbors the conception of an ecumenical movement, providing for collaboration on specific matters across lines of difference. Voluntary and limited association rather than a superorganization should be the goal. In the area of voluntary cooperation a better spirit is evident in American Jewry.[39] Organizations of more limited scope and membership have proved more viable than attempts to impose a monolithic order. So, in various localities, rabbis of widely differing positions have been able to unite on common programs. Support of institutions of higher Jewish learning has come from all camps. Still, in spite of such scattered successes, the summary statement must be that the American Jew is a jealous congregationalist.

If this is so, it is relevant to ask what he has made of his congregations. Here the distinctive institutional form of American Jewish life begins to come clearly into view. The typical Jewish congregation houses a wide variety of non-religious and semireligious activities, as well as serving religious functions. Sabbath and Holy Day services are held; there may also be weekday services. There are study groups in which Jewish learning on various levels is pursued. There is a Sunday school; there often is also a weekday Hebrew school. There are a men's club and a women's club, a younger members' group, social and athletic groups for teenagers (perhaps a gymnasium). There are sewing groups and card-playing groups, boy scouts and girl scouts. Local Zionist activities may center in the synagogue building. Dances at Purim, or, more recently, at the conclusion of the Day of Atonement, may take place there. This, in epitome, is the American synagogue today. It serves a great many worthy purposes and requires efficient programming and administration. Its defect is that of many institutions in the modern world; it requires plenty of committees and very little commitment.

As an unconsciously evolved phenomenon of American Jewish life the synagogue-center, as a substitute for the community, can certainly be traced back to the early years of the twentieth century and may even have begun to take its characteristic form at the end of the nineteenth century. As a conscious program, however, the concept of the synagogue-center was formulated by Mordecai Kaplan in 1918. Kaplan surely did not anticipate that the Jewish center that he proposed would become a focus for the conflict of "religious" and "secular" forces in American Jewish life; yet it has, in fact, become so. Its most ardent proponents have been the secular welfare groups, especially the National Jewish Welfare Board. Opposition has most often come from leaders of rabbinical thought. Rabbi Israel Goldstein, for example, speaking before the Rabbinical Assembly in 1929, caustically criticized the synagogue-center: "No doubt there is much to be said in its favor, but it is true, as has been repeatedly stated by its critics, that whereas the hope of the Synagogue Center was to synagogize the tone of the secular activities of the family, the effect has been the secularization of the place of the Synagogue." [40] To the same effect, Rabbi Abba Hillel Silver wrote, "The crowding of many secular activities in the life of a congregation frequently causes men to lose sight of the real purposes of a religious organization." [41] More recently, discussing a different proposal stemming from the National Jewish Welfare Board in 1949, Rabbi David Aronson, then president of the Rabbinical Assembly, echoed these earlier comments in saying, "A community that accepts the philosophy that a gymnasium is as essential to Jewish life as a synagogue, and a Jewish basketball team as conducive to Jewish survival as a Talmud Torah [Jewish school], is on its way to Jewish extinction." [42]

On the other hand, Kaplan has maintained that the difficulties stem from the failure of the rabbis to use the synagogue-center properly, and not from the nature of the synagogue-center itself.

Opportunity has brought to the Rabbi the institution of the Jewish Center. If he had only known how to utilize it, he could have made of it the means to a Jewish spiritual and cultural renaissance. But lacking the training in the human sciences, he regards it merely as a means of inveigling the young people to the synagogue.[43]

A social worker, Harry L. Glucksman, director of the National Jewish Welfare Board, thought that it was the non-synagogal functions that suffered in the synagogue-center. They were, he said, "shunted to an insignificant location and frequently relegated to the position of an annex to the synagogue." This happened because "the Synagogue proper and its accessories had prior claims on the building funds," so that the amount available for center facilities was always inadequate.[44]

While the "secular" and "religious" doctors have thus disagreed in their diagnoses of the nature of the ailment, the synagogue-center movement, whether identified by this name or not, has met a need in the life of the Jews of America and has, therefore, kept on growing. More and more congregations have invested in new buildings and transformed themselves into Jewish centers. Whether the rabbis supported the move or not, they have been compelled to go along, even while they may have been wondering whether, in attempting to do all things and to be all things, the American synagogue has not allowed its major functions to lapse into relative insignificance. Whatever the rabbis may like, the dominant laity likes the synagogue-center. Since the American synagogue is lay-controlled, it becomes what the laity makes of it. In the eighteenth century the Jewish laity strove to make each synagogue a community; in the twentieth century they are proud to have made it a community center.

## WHAT HAS HAPPENED TO JEWISH RELIGION?

Almost two centuries have elapsed since European Enlightenment and the emancipation of the Jews which ensued produced a crisis in Jewish religion. Pressures, both from within the Jewish people and from the surrounding culture, impelled the Jews to alter, modify, and adapt the ancient traditions of the Jewish religion and make them more suitable as guides to living in a modern ambience. The need stirred dormant powers of creativity in the Jewish spirit. An exciting literature, unmatched since the previous great age of crisis, the adjustment to Europe in the middle ages, came to the birth. The chief institutional forms developed to meet previous crises—the Jewish community and the synagogue—were radically altered. Many new programs were proposed, and institutions embodying these programs were established. Those that seem, from our limited historical perspective, the most important of these programs have been examined here. I have tried to show both their relation to the previous history of Jewish religion and their responsiveness to the environment in which they were proposed. What remains is to try to indicate what has happened in the last few decades by way of further modification that may affect our appraisal of what emancipation has made of Jewish religion.

The most noteworthy conditions that must enter into the account are these. The Jewish communities of Central Europe, in which many of the impulses that have been described here were first discerned, are now all but wiped out. In addition, in the Communist countries of Eastern Europe, Jewish life has been undermined to so great an extent that it is in decline. To counterbalance these tremendous losses, the Jews of the United States now constitute the major center of Jewish life in dispersion, and a Jewish State has been reestablished in Israel, with tolerable prospects of continuing unless there is a major realignment of world forces. The environing world is one in which war, rather than peace, has come to seem the normal state of human society. Men are conceived as responding more to irrational forces than to their own reason. Traditionalism and sentimentalism are on the rise; civilization is widely considered a precariously thin veneer concealing primitive barbarism. In the classic phrase that Sidney Hook drew from Gilbert Murray, the midtwentieth century is experiencing a "failure of nerve." [45]

Reform Judaism in recent years has manifested the influence of this twentieth-century shift to the right by its retreat from the more extreme principles of the nineteenth century as expressed in the Pittsburgh Platform. In part this is a consequence of the belated entry of Eastern European Jews into the leadership of the Reform Movement. These "new" Reformers brought with them a sharper sense of the spiritual and esthetic satisfactions of a more traditional approach to ritual than the nineteenth-century, Western European founders of the Reform Movement had. Under their stimulus Reform Judaism has moved far closer to a Conservative orientation than would have seemed possible a generation ago. The shift is particularly noticeable in the ritual of the synagogue and in the return to some of the traditional home ceremonies (a reversal of the trend to the institutional Passover Seder, lighting of the Sabbath candles, etc.). It may also be observed by noting the differences between the 1885 Pittsburgh Platform and the 1937 program of Reform Judaism. The later document reveals the new century's renewed regard for the customary and the traditional.

Reform Judaism's 1937 program showed the effect of the half-century that had elapsed since Pittsburgh by announcing itself merely as a set of "Guiding Principles of Reform Judaism," rather than as a creedal platform. The Guiding Principles, while maintaining some of the self-conscious universalism of the older Platform, introduce a note of particularism by defining Judaism as the "historical religious experience of the Jewish people." Then, after an affirmation of strict monotheism and transcendence, and a statement that man is a being with free will and an immortal soul, the Guiding Principles go on to assert that the Torah is revealed truth, not in the sense of literal inspiration, but in terms of the belief that "revelation is a continuous process." However, "each age has the obligation to adapt the teachings of the *Torah* to its basic needs in consonance with the genius of Judaism." This is a far more traditional approach than that of 1885, and differs verbally but little from the sort of statement that would be acceptable to a Conservative, or even a Neo-Orthodox, group.

The clearest indication of Reform Judaism's renewed regard for tradition comes in the third major section of the Guiding Principles, dealing with religious practice. Here it is asserted that Jewish life "calls for faithful participation in the life of the Jewish community as it finds expression in home, synagogue, and school and in all other agencies that enrich Jewish life and promote its welfare." A few words are devoted to expanding on the conceptions of home, synagogue, and school. Then a paragraph is given to prayer, "the voice of religion, the language of hope and aspiration." It is asserted that "to deepen the spiritual life of our people, we must cultivate the traditional habit of communion with God through prayer in both home and synagogue," a view that the elders in 1885 felt it unnecessary to record. Toward the close of the section on religious practice, this paragraph appears:

Judaism as a way of life requires in addition to its moral and spiritual demands, the preservation of the Sabbath, festivals and Holy Days, the retention and development of such customs, symbols and ceremonies as possess inspirational value, the cultivation of distinctive forms of religious art and music, and the use of Hebrew, together with the vernacular, in our worship and instruction.[46]

In addition, as we have seen earlier, the Reform Movement shifted its position to accommodate Zionism. The differences between the 1937 Guiding Principles and the Pittsburgh Platform are so great that the two documents seem scarcely to proceed from the same movement.

The major change in Orthodoxy we have already discussed, namely, the shift from traditional supernatural Messianism to at least an acceptance of cooperation with the political Zionist movement. One consequence of this has been the readiness of Orthodox groups [47] to participate in the government of the State of Israel and to submit to the authority of the Israeli Chief Rabbinate. In part this willingness may stem from the fact that the Orthodox parties have virtually the status of an established church in Israel. Indeed, with respect to its Jewish citizens, Israel does not maintain freedom of religion. Thus, the law of that State requires the official leadership of any religious group to designate those persons who are authorized to perform marriages, while making no provision at all for civil marriage ceremonies. The Chief Rabbi names only Orthodox rabbis; as a result, no Jew can be married in Israel unless he is willing to tolerate an Orthodox ceremony. Since no Orthodox rabbi will solemnize a marriage if its conditions in any way violate the traditional rabbinical laws, certain otherwise acceptable unions are barred by the refusal of the authorized rabbis to perform the ceremony. The Orthodox groups have been able to prevent the application of one section of the Defence Service Law of 1949 which made women as well as men subject to military training. They have forced the government to adopt extremely rigorous Sabbath observance laws. Their opposition prevented for some time the erection of a Reform synagogue in Jerusalem, although the municipal council had approved its building.

Because of the stranglehold that the Orthodox parties have on Judaism in Israel, most of the Israelis are secularists. Probably less than fifteen percent of the population is actively religious; the rest is indifferent. Thus far in Israel's modern history, however, the tail has wagged the dog, and is still unsatisfied because the entire house does not move. One of Israel's Chief Rabbis, Isaac Herzog, declared:

The aim of Orthodox Jewry in Israel is to bring about a state law which will make the law of the Torah binding. It must be pointed out that even at present [1949] one of the basic laws of the state must be the observation of the Sabbath and Kashrut [dietary laws]. And we hope that with God's help the law of our Jewish State will be based on the tenets of the Torah.[48]

In the same article Herzog insisted on the need for the civil law of marriage and divorce to conform to the rabbinical law, even though he acknowledged that "this may eventually bring about a racial split between orthodox and non-orthodox Jewry and prevent intermarriage between them." [49] Representatives of other than Orthodox interpretations of Judaism maintain that the abstention of more than four out of five Israelis from religious activities is not an expression of a positive antagonism to religion, but only of a determination to resist the imposition of the Orthodox conception upon everyone. If Conservative and Reform synagogues were available, they claim, many of those who are now indifferent would adhere to these more liberal forms. To this the Orthodox reply that Jewish religion, in its traditional rabbinic form, is the only bond that unites the immigrants from all over the world, and in establishing a new nation it is vital that there should be such a bond.[50]

In the United States, the other major center of Jewish life, it is still the case that the Orthodox synagogues have the largest membership. Mere numerical predominance does not, however, tell the story, for, as Marshall Sklare pointed out, a considerable segment of its membership does not, in fact, observe the traditional code. He uses the term "Non-observant Orthodox Jew" to describe one who is "heterodox in personal behavior but who, when occasionally joining in public worship, prefers to do so in accordance with traditional patterns." [51] Salo W. Baron reports "the general superficiality of Orthodox allegiance," and specifies these charges: "Many so-called Orthodox Jews are outright sinners before the Law, breaking the Sabbath rest commandment, taking lightly the dietary provisions, neglecting their stated prayers, and generally living in a way which would have appeared as an abomination to their East European ancestors." [52] Sklare notes other defections from traditional law, especially neglect of the laws of female purification, one of only three categorical obligations of women in the rabbinical system:

The female purifications are not widely practiced. A *mikveh* (ritual bath) is located in the neighborhood, but it is patronized only by a handful. From the viewpoint of the sacred system, most of the young and middle-aged married women in the community commit a major sin by not observing the laws of purification. However, their ritual uncleanliness is not only generally disregarded, but in many circles the very concept has become a subject for cynicism and humor. Such a reaction is understandable toward a tradition which varies so widely from Western religious norms: according to such norms impurity results from a *moral* rather than a ritualistic transgression.[53]

Apart from these critical views, it should be noted that in the last few years, during which the "swing to the right" has been so prominent, Orthodox Judaism has drawn into its ranks many young people, who are almost ostentatious in their display of the external manifestations of ritual observance. How permanent this youth movement will be is impossible to predict; if it is a consequence of the uncertainty facing the young in the world of today, it may persist as long as that uncertainty.[54]

Within the Conservative group there are no significant changes to be reported for the latest period. It may still be described as a movement in which rabbis who are a shade to the left of Orthodoxy minister to congregations a shade to the right of Reform. Under the wing of Conservative Judaism (its left wing), however, a new development, most consciously of the twentieth century, has been started. This is the Reconstructionist movement, an institutional expression of the philosophic and theological ideas of Mordecai Kaplan. Reconstructionism may best be understood if we begin with a statement of fact and continue with a supposition. The statement of fact is this: self-conscious awareness of the principles upon which change takes place is a relatively recent phenomenon of the human mind. Partly this is the consequence of a tendency prevalent in philosophy from the time of the ancient Greeks to the nineteenth century to search for ultimate Reality in the permanent and unchanging, while more recent philosophy has inclined to regard change as the essence of the Real. Partly it has been the result of the emergence, quite recently, of the social sciences, with their focus on the dynamics of change. The supposition is this: if we can bring to bear on religion our new sophisticated understanding of the principles of change, our knowledge of modern philosophy, and both the theoretical knowledge and the applied techniques of social science, we shall be able to make more rapid, more conscious, more deliberate adaptations of Judaism to contemporary conditions and needs than could be made in the past, when these changes came about only as the result of the operation of forces of which the Jews were not conscious. This supposition is the basic principle of the Reconstructionist point of view in contemporary Judaism. Reconstructionism is self-consciously modern, unabashed in its reference to the social sciences, and grounded in an explicit philosophy of Jewish existence. The leaders of the Reconstructionist movement are hospitable to change, not so much for its own sake as for the sake of the continuity of the Jewish people and of Jewish civilization. As we have seen in the discussion of Mordecai Kaplan's thought, Reconstructionism welcomes changes in interpretation more readily than changes in practice. It attempts to be true to tradition where tradition helps to sanctify present-day life, without being in thrall to tradition. Neither a sweeping acceptance nor an equally sweeping rejection of tradition is desirable, for some traditions have retained their vitality and other traditions have not. To know which is which, however, requires conscientious study of the documents in which both the vital and the moribund traditions are preserved, as well as study of those modern philosophies and scientific disciplines that can help to distinguish between the vital and the moribund. Reconstructionism, therefore, demands a dedication to study, an intellectual awareness of contemporary currents of thought, and a readiness to make and to live by one's own informed judgments.

As an organized movement in twentieth-century Jewish life, Reconstructionism has not made the gains that its founders hoped. Perhaps the reason is that it has not adequately reckoned with the retreat from reason, for, despite its grounding in a nonrational philosophy, Reconstructionism is essentially a reasonable faith for reasonable men. Thus far it has not had to face the most difficult question: whether it is more than an instrument for the experimental testing of the ideas of Mordecai Kaplan. If it can develop into more than this, it may be an important movement in twenty-first-century Judaism. If it cannot, at least its central principle, that of conscious and deliberate change, will surely survive and have a long career as an element in the thought and practice of the leaders of both Reform and Conservative Judaism.

Judaism is the oldest of the major religions in the West. Even though it has never been the religion of any major fragment of the population of the world, its ancient history has been of great interest to students of the history of religion because of its creativity and innovative power. Because of this force within it, Judaism has been the seedbed of other religions, Christianity and Islam in particular. Yet the modern history of Judaism has been too little studied, on the assumption, perhaps, that its creative phase lies in the past. If this were true, Judaism would, indeed, be a vestigial religion,[55] a survival from a past in which it was viable into a present in which it has no vital function. But it is not true. Judaism is still able to respond creatively to the novel situations in which the Jews find themselves; it is still a living faith.

Here I have examined some of the chief attempts, both on the theoretical and on the institutional level, within Judaism to come to grips with the novelties amid which Jewish life has been lived during the past two centuries. These are essays in giving direction to Jewish religion under conditions of emancipation. Their very diversity is an indication of strength, not of weakness. It is a sign of ferment, and ferment is the very stuff of life. None of the ways just examined may prove ultimately to be a successful adjustment between Judaism and modernity, but that so many ways should have been proposed is a warrant for the belief that a successful way will be found.

# Notes

## NOTES TO CHAPTER 1: EMANCIPATION AND THE BIRTH OF MODERN JUDAISM

1. Cf. Israel Abrahams, *Jewish Life in the Middle Ages* (Philadelphia, The Jewish Publication Society of America, 1896), pp. 399–412; Malcolm Hay, *The Foot of Pride: The Pressure of Christendom on the People of Israel for 1900 Years* (Boston, Beacon Press, 1950); and James Parkes, *The Conflict of the Church and the Synagogue* (London, The Soncino Press, 1934).

2. Ferdinand Gregorovius, *The Ghetto and the Jews of Rome*, tr. Moses Hadas (New York, Schocken Books, 1948), pp. 45–79; Louis Wirth, *The Ghetto* (Chicago, University of Chicago Press, 1928), pp. 15–18.

3. Joshua Trachtenberg, *The Devil and the Jews: The Medieval Conception of the Jew and Its Relation to Modern Anti-Semitism* (New Haven, Yale University Press, 1943), pp. 32–43, 44–52.

4. Salo Wittmayer Baron, *A Social and Religious History of the Jews* (New York, Columbia University Press, 1937), III, 96–99, nn. 5–8.

5. Abrahams, *Jewish Life*, pp. 234 ff.; for further detail, see Aaron Friedenwald, "Jewish Physicians and the Contributions of the Jews to the Science of Medicine," *Publications* (Gratz College), I (1897), 107–65; for a chronological treatment of the role of Jewish physicians in Italy from the Jews' first settlement to 1870, see also Harry Friedenwald, "Jewish Physicians in Italy: Their Relation to the Papal and Italian States," in *The Jews and Medi-*

*cine: Essays* (Baltimore, Johns Hopkins Press, 1944), II, 551–612.

6. Henry Sumner Maine, *Ancient Law* (New York, Henry Holt, 1873), pp. 128–63.

7. See Guido Kisch, *Jewry-Law in Medieval Germany: Laws and Court Decisions Concerning Jews* (New York, American Academy for Jewish Research, 1949); see also G. Kisch, *The Jews in Medieval Germany: A Study of Their Legal and Social Status* (Chicago, University of Chicago Press, 1949).

8. Salo W. Baron, *The Jewish Community* (Philadelphia, Jewish Publication Society, 1948), II, 209.

9. *Ibid.,* II, 3–51.

10. J. W. Thompson, *Economic and Social History of Europe in the Later Middle Ages* (New York and London, The Century Co., 1931), pp. 378–95.

11. Cf. Clough and Cole, *Economic History of Europe* (Boston, Heath, 1946), especially ch. IV, "Capitalists of the New Spirit."

12. Maine, *Ancient Law,* p. 165.

13. Cecil Roth, *The Jews in the Renaissance* (Philadelphia, Jewish Publication Society, 1959), pp. 23 f.

14. *Ibid.,* pp. 112–21, 156 f. See also Eugenio Anagnine, *G. Pico della Mirandola: Sincretismo religioso-filosofico 1463–1494* (Bari, Laterza e Figli, 1937); Eugenio Garin, *Pico della Mirandola, vita e dottrina* (Firenze, Felice LeMonnier, 1937); Egidio de Viterbo, *Scechina e Libellus de litteris Hebraicis,* ed. François Secret (Roma, Centro Internazionale di Studi Umanisti, 1959), especially the introduction; and F. Secret, *Les kabbalistes chrétiens de la Renaissance* (Paris, Dunod, 1964), pp. 24–43.

15. Ellis Rivkin, *Leon da Modena and the Kol Sakhal* (Cincinnati, Hebrew Union College Press, 1952), p. 25, n. 27.

16. Roth, *The Jews in the Renaissance,* pp. 288–99; *Grove's Dictionary of Music and Musicians* (5th ed.), ed. Eric Blom (London, Macmillan, 1954), VII, 243 f.; Abraham Z. Idelsohn, *Jewish Music in Its Historical Development* (New York, Henry Holt, 1929), pp. 196–203.

17. Roth, *The Jews in the Renaissance,* p. 293.

18. Abrahams, *Jewish Life,* pp. 390 ff.

19. Roth, *The Jews in the Renaissance,* p. 26.

20. *Ibid.*

21. *Ibid.,* p. 27; Rivkin, *Leon da Modena,* p. 28, n. 35.

22. See Simon Dubnow, *Weltgeschichte des jüdischen Volkes,* tr. A. Steinberg (Berlin, Jüdischer Verlag, 1927), VI, 85 ff.

23. Roth, *The Jews in the Renaissance,* p. 14. The term "counter-Renaissance" is used by Hiram Haydn in his most suggestive book, *The Counter-Renaisssance* (New York, Scribners, 1950).

24. Baron, *The Jewish Community,* I, 255–59; see also H. S. Q. Henriques, *The Jews and English Law* (London, J. Jacobs, 1908), pp. 125 ff.

25. Italics in original. See *Journals of the House of Commons,* A1662 [N.S.1663] 15 [error for 14] Car II [Die] Jovis, 26 Feb., for the resolution to appoint a committee (p. 441) and Die Mercurii 8 Aprilis 14 Car II Regis 1663, for debate on the proposed resolution (p. 468) which was not adopted. See also Cecil Roth, *A History of the Jews in England* (Oxford, Clarendon Press, 1941), p. 170.

26. Montesquieu, *The Spirit of Laws,* tr. Thomas Nugent (New York, Colonial Press, 1900), Book I, sec. 1, p. 2.

27. Immanuel Kant, *Foundations of the Metaphysics of Morals* and *What is Enlightenment?* tr. Lewis White Beck (Chicago, University of Chicago Press, 1950), pp. 286, 291.

28. Baron, *A Social and Religious History of the Jews,* III, 142, n. 15; Cecil Roth, "The Jews of Western Europe (from 1648)," in L. Finkelstein, ed., *The Jews, Their History, Culture, and Religion* (Philadelphia, Jewish Publication Society, 1949), I, 261 ff., 264–66.

29. Joseph L. Blau and Salo W. Baron, *The Jews of the United States, 1790–1840: A Documentary History* (New York, Columbia University Press, 1963), I, 60, 248, n. 101; 64, 249, n. 109; xxii f.

30. For biographical data on Mendelssohn, see Hermann Walter, *Moses Mendelssohn, Critic and Philosopher* (New York, Bloch, 1930).

31. *Solomon Maimon: An Autobiography,* ed. Moses Hadas (New York, Schocken Books, 1947), p. 96.

32. As translated in W. Gunther Plaut, *The Rise of Reform Judaism* (New York, World Union for Progressive Judaism, Ltd., 1963), p. 6, from Moses Mendelssohn, "Jerusalem," Part II, in *Gesammelte Schriften* (Leipzig, 1843), III, 311 ff.

33. Mendelssohn, *Gesammelte Schriften* (Leipzig, 1843), II. See first dialogue, pp. 99–138, for a Leibnizian proof; see the end of the work, for a Platonic discussion. See also Jacob B. Agus, *The Evolution of Jewish Thought from Biblical Times to the Opening of the Modern Era* (London, Abelard-Schuman, 1959), pp. 384 f.

34. W. Gunther Plaut, *The Rise of Reform Judaism* (New York, World Union for Progressive Judaism, Ltd., 1963), pp. 7 f., from translation in *Hebrew Review,* N.S. (London, 1859), I, 51 ff.

35. Translated by Plaut, *Rise of Reform Judaism,* p. 13, from *Sulamith* (Leipzig, 1806), I, 9.

36. *Sulamith,* VI (1822?), no. 2, pp. 8–18, parts of which are quoted in Blau and Baron, *The Jews of the United States,* I, 88–93; see also p. 256 f., n. 181.

37. Roth, *A Short History of the Jewish People* (London, East and West Library, 1948), pp. 339 f.
38. Mendelssohn, *Jerusalem* (Berlin, 1783), Part II, p. 140, n.: "Leider! hören wir auch schon den Congress in Amerika das alte Lied anstimmen, und von einer *herrschenden Religion* sprechen."
39. Roth, *Short History*, p. 341.
40. See Georges Lefebvre, *The Coming of the French Revolution*, tr. R. R. Palmer (Princeton University Press, 1947), pp. 221–23, for text, pp. 169–81, especially p. 174, for discussion.
41. Salo W. Baron, "The Modern Age," in *Great Ages and Ideas of the Jewish People*, ed. Leo W. Schwarz (New York, Modern Library, 1956), pp. 323 ff.; Roth, *Short History*, p. 341.
42. Roth, *Short History*, pp. 341–43.
43. Mendelssohn, "Jerusalem," *Gesammelte Schriften* (Leipzig, 1843), III, 358 ff.

NOTES TO CHAPTER 2: THE INITIAL RESPONSE: REFORM
JUDAISM IN EUROPE AND AMERICA

1. Israel Abrahams, *Jewish Life in the Middle Ages* (Philadelphia, The Jewish Publication Society of America, 1896), p. 418. See also Heinrich Graetz, *History of the Jews* (Philadelphia, Jewish Publication Society, 1894), IV, 215 f., for a discussion of the efforts of the anti-pope Benedict XIII to harass the Jews. The German edition of Graetz's *History* (VIII, 123) cites a reference to the 1425 bull of Benedict in Bartolocci, *Bibliotheca Rabbinica*, III, 731 ff.
2. Cecil Roth, *A Short History of the Jewish People* (London, East and West Library, 1948), p. 375.
3. See Abraham Z. Idelsohn, *Jewish Music in its Historical Development* (New York, Henry Holt, 1929), pp. 7–21, and Eric Werner, "Jewish Music," in *Grove's Dictionary of Music and Musicians* (5th ed.), ed. Eric Blom, IV, 615–36, especially "Music in the Bible," pp. 616–21. Idelsohn cites as biblical evidence for the trumpet Numbers 10:1–10; for cymbals, Ezra 2:41, 3:10; for a flute, Psalm 150:4; for a double-pipe, I Chronicles 15:20; for bells, Exodus 28:35; and as Talmudic evidence for a pipe organ (*magrepha*), Mishna Tamid V:6 and B. Arachin 10b. See also Peter Crossley-Holland, "Non-Western Music," sect. 9, "The Jews," in *The Pelican History of Music*, ed. Alec Robertson and Denis Stevens (Penguin Books, c. 1960), I, 104–11.
4. Cecil Roth, *The Jews in the Renaissance* (Philadelphia, The Jewish Publication Society, 1959), pp. 271 f. Note also the following comment by Samuel Pepys on his visit to a service for Simhat Torah

(Rejoicing in the Law) at the Sephardic synagogue in London, entry of October 14, 1663: "After dinner my wife and I to the Jewish Synagogue, where the men and boys in their vayles, and the women behind a lattice out of sight; and some things stand up, which I believe is their Law, in a press to which all coming in do bow; and at the putting on of their vayles do say something, to which others that hear him do cry Amen, and the party do kiss his vayle. Their service all in a singing way, and in Hebrew. And anon their Laws that they take out of the press are carried by several men, four or five several burthens in all, and they do relieve one another; and (whether it is that every one desires to have the carrying of it I cannot tell), thus they carried it around the room while such a service is singing. And in the end they had a prayer for the King, which they pronounced his name in Portugall; but the prayer, like the rest, in Hebrew. But, Lord! to see the disorder, laughing, sporting, and no attention, but confusion in all their service, more like brutes than people knowing the true God, would make a man forswear ever seeing them more. Away thence with my mind strongly disturbed with them." *Everybody's Pepys: The Diary of Samuel Pepys 1660–1669,* ed. Ernest H. Shepard (New York, Harcourt, Brace, 1926), p. 209.

5. David Philipson, *The Reform Movement in Judaism* (New York, Macmillan, 1907), pp. 23 ff. See also W. Gunther Plaut, *The Rise of Reform Judaism* (New York, World Union for Progressive Judaism, Ltd., 1963), pp. 158–60, from Zunz, *Die gottesdienstliche Vorträge der Juden,* as translated in *Hebrew Review* (London, 1859), N.S. I, 472 ff., and *Archives Israélites,* I, 234, and II, 197 f.

6. Hermann Walter, *Moses Mendelssohn, Critic and Philosopher* (New York, Bloch, 1930), pp. 146 f.; Jacob B. Agus, *The Evolution of Jewish Thought from Biblical Times to the Opening of the Modern Era* (London, Abelard-Schuman, 1959), pp. 372–80.

7. Plaut, *Rise of Reform Judaism,* p. 11, from David Friedländer, *Sendschreiben an . . . Probst Teller* (Berlin, 1799), p. 61.

8. Philipson, *The Reform Movement,* p. 12, from I. M. Jost, *Geschichte der Israeliten,* IX, 120.

9. See Philipson, *The Reform Movement,* pp. 19–22.

10. *Ibid.,* p. 21.

11. Plaut, *Rise of Reform Judaism,* p. 29, from Israel Jacobson Dedication Address, *Sulamith,* third year (1810), I, 298 ff.

12. Philipson, *The Reform Movement,* pp. 42 f.

13. *Ibid.,* p. 33, n. 3.

14. Plaut, *Rise of Reform Judaism,* p. 32; Philipson, *The Reform Movement,* pp. 45 f.

15. Plaut, *Rise of Reform Judaism*, p. 31, from *Theologische Gutachten über das Gebetbuch nach dem Gebrauche des neuen israelitischen Tempelvereine in Hamburg* (Hamburg, 1842), pp. 4–5.

16. Plaut, *Rise of Reform Judaism*, p. 31.

17. *Ibid.*, pp. 16 f.

18. Salo W. Baron, "The Modern Age," in *Great Ages and Ideas of the Jewish People,* ed. Leo W. Schwarz (New York, Modern Library, 1956), p. 382; on Jost, see Baron, "I. M. Jost the Historian," in *History and Jewish Historians,* ed. Arthur Hertzberg and Leon A. Feldman (Philadelphia, Jewish Publication Society, 1964), pp. 240–62 (originally printed in *Proceedings* of the American Academy for Jewish Research [New York, 1928–30], pp. 7–32).

19. See Philipson, *The Reform Movement,* pp. 33–41; Baron, "The Modern Age," in *Great Ages and Ideas,* p. 382; Emil G. Hirsch, "Leopold Zunz," in *The Jewish Encyclopedia,* XII, 699–704.

20. Jacob B. Agus, *Modern Philosophies of Judaism: A Study of Recent Jewish Philosophies of Religion* (New York, Behrman's Jewish Book House, 1941), pp. 11–16; Isidore Singer, "Solomon Ludwig Steinheim (Levy)," in *The Jewish Encyclopedia,* XI, 543 f.

21. See Philipson, *The Reform Movement,* pp. 88–92.

22. *Ibid.*, p. 180, n. 1 (quoted from Wilhelm Freund, ed., *Zur Juedenfrage in Deutschland* [Breslau, 1843–44], II, 165 f.).

23. Philipson, *The Reform Movement,* p. 43, n. 1 (quoted from Holdheim, *Das Ceremonialgesetz in Messiasreich* [Schwerin, 1845], p. 50).

24. Abraham Geiger, *Das Judenthum und seine Geschichte, bis zur Zerstörung des zweiten Tempels* (Breslau, 1865), I, 9.

25. *Ibid.*, pp. 13 f.

26. Agus, *Modern Philosophies of Judaism,* pp. 5–11; Joseph L. Blau, *The Story of Jewish Philosophy* (New York, Random House, 1962), pp. 269–75; Philipson, *The Reform Movement,* pp. 64–68 and *passim.*

27. See, for example, documents in Joseph L. Blau and Salo W. Baron, *The Jews of the United States, 1790–1840: A Documentary History* (New York, Columbia University Press, 1963), vol. II: for attempts by several congregations to cooperate in Hebraic education, pp. 585, 586 f.; on the synagogue's role in dietary matters, pp. 524–28; on other questions of Jewish law, pp. 588 ff.; for the role of Congregation Shearith Israel in New York City in burial arrangements, p. 518; and on synagogal philanthropic activities, pp. 591 f.

28. Blau and Baron, *The Jews of the United States,* II, 554. See also Philipson, *The Reform Movement,* pp. 466 ff.

29. Philipson, *The Reform Movement,* pp. 462 f.

30. Blau and Baron, *The Jews of the United States,* II, 560.

31. Reprinted in Blau and Baron, *The Jews of the United States,* III, 706–10, from *North American Review,* XXIII (July, 1826), 67–69.

32. Philipson, *The Reform Movement,* pp. 464 f.

33. Blau and Baron, *The Jews of the United States,* III, 704 f., reprinted from L. C. Moise, *Biography of Isaac Harby* (Columbia, S.C., Bryan, 1931), p. 95.

34. Blau and Baron, *The Jews of the United States,* II, 658, n. 146, from Moise, *Biography of Isaac Harby,* p. 126.

35. Blau and Baron, *The Jews of the United States,* III, 710, from *North American Review,* XXIII (July, 1826), 69.

36. Philipson, *The Reform Movement,* pp. 466 ff.

37. *Ibid.,* pp. 197–99.

38. *Ibid.,* pp. 72–101.

39. *Ibid.,* p. 75.

40. Quoted in Philipson, *The Reform Movement,* p. 76.

41. Quoted *ibid.,* p. 78.

42. Quoted *ibid.,* pp. 84 f.

43. Joseph Abraham Friedländer, rabbi of Westphalia, in *Rabbinische Gutachten über die Verträglichkeit der freien Forschung mit dem Rabbineramte* (September, 1842), I, 4; quoted in Philipson, *The Reform Movement,* p. 86.

44. *Rabbinische Gutachten,* I, 9; quoted in Philipson, *The Reform Movement,* pp. 86 f.

45. For a discussion of the conferences, see Philipson, *The Reform Movement,* pp. 200–316; for documents pertaining thereto, cf. Plaut, *Rise of Reform Judaism,* pp. 74–90.

46. For references on the oath *more Judaico,* see Salo W. Baron, *The Jewish Community* (Philadelphia, Jewish Publication Society, 1948), III, 180 f.

47. Philipson, *The Reform Movement,* p. 315.

48. Hyman B. Grinstein, *The Rise of the Jewish Community of New York* (Philadelphia, Jewish Publication Society, 1945), p. 90; and Philipson, *The Reform Movement,* p. 469.

49. Philipson, *The Reform Movement,* p. 469.

50. For discussions of Wise, see Philipson, *The Reform Movement,* pp. 469 f., 477–79; Israel Knox, *Rabbi in America: The Story of Isaac M. Wise* (Boston, Little, Brown, 1957); and M. B. May, *Isaac Mayer Wise, the Founder of American Judaism: A Biography* (New York, Putnam, 1916).

51. Philipson, *The Reform Movement,* pp. 475–77.

52. *Ibid.,* pp. 470 f.
53. *Ibid.,* p. 471.
54. *Ibid.,* pp. 479–85.
55. *Ibid.,* pp. 485–87.
56. *Ibid.,* pp. 483 f.
57. *Ibid.,* p. 473.
58. Theodore Parker, "The Transient and Permanent in Christianity," delivered at Hawes Place Church in Boston, May 19, 1841, reprinted in *The Transient and the Permanent in Christianity* (Boston, American Unitarian Association, 1908 [volume IV of *The Works of Theodore Parker*], pp. 1–39; nn. pp. 447–50.
59. Philipson, *The Reform Movement,* p. 476.
60. *Ibid.,* p. 479.
61. *Ibid.,* p. 480.
62. *Ibid.*
63. *Ibid.,* p. 484.
64. *Ibid.,* p. 485.
65. *Occident,* IV (1846–47), 475.
66. Moshe Davis, *The Emergence of Conservative Judaism: The Historical School in 19th Century America* (Philadelphia, Jewish Publication Society, 1963), pp. 175–81, 219–20; Philipson, *The Reform Movement,* pp. 510 f.
67. Davis, *Emergence of Conservative Judaism,* pp. 224 f.; Albert H. Friedlander, *Reform Judaism in America: The Pittsburgh Platform* (New York, Union of American Hebrew Congregations, 1958), pp. 13–19; Beryl H. Levy, *Reform Judaism in America: A Study in Religious Adaptation* (New York, Bloch, 1933), for the Kohler-Kohut controversy, pp. 57–60; for the Pittsburgh Conference, pp. 60–69.
68. Philipson, *The Reform Movement,* pp. 488–91.
69. *Ibid.,* p. 491.
70. Lou Silberman, "The Recent History of Reform Philosophy," *Yearbook of the Central Conference of American Rabbis,* LXIII (1953), 285; quoted in Friedlander, *Reform Judaism in America,* p. 8.
71. *Proceedings of the Pittsburg Rabbinical Conference* (Central Conference of American Rabbis, 1923), pp. 7 f.
72. Text in Philipson, *The Reform Movement,* pp. 491 f.
73. See Joseph L. Blau, "An American-Jewish View of the Evolution Controversy," in *Hebrew Union College Annual* (Cincinnati, 1947), XX, 617–34; cf. Joseph Krauskopf, *Evolution and Judaism* (Kansas City, Berkowitz & Co., 1887).

NOTES TO CHAPTER 3: REFORMULATING JEWISH
ORTHODOXY: SAMSON RAPHAEL HIRSCH AND HIS SUCCESSORS

1. See S. M. Dubnow, *History of the Jews in Russia and Poland from the Earliest Times until the Present Day* (Philadelphia, Jewish Publication Society, 1918); and S. W. Baron, *The Russian Jew under Tsars and Soviets* (New York, Macmillan, 1964).

2. See Abraham Joshua Heschel, *The Earth is the Lord's: The Inner World of the Jew in Eastern Europe* (New York, Henry Schuman, 1950).

3. For discussions of the Hassidim, see Samuel H. Dresner, *The Zaddik: The Doctrine of the Zaddik According to the Writings of Rabbi Yaakov Yosef of Polnoy* (London, Abelard-Schuman, 1960); Solomon Schechter, "The Chassidim," in *Studies in Judaism: First Series* (Philadelphia, Jewish Publication Society, 1945); and the numerous writings on the subject by Martin Buber. For a popularized treatment of the movement, see Jacob S. Minkin, *The Romance of Hassidism* (New York, Yoseloff, 1955); and for a collection of Hassidic writings, see *The Hasidic Anthology*, ed. Louis I. Newman (New York, Bloch, 1944).

4. Philipson, *The Reform Movement in Judaism* (New York, Macmillan, 1907), p. 82. This statement is, of course, extreme; it was sent as one of the replies on Rabbi Tiktin's behalf in the Geiger-Tiktin controversy discussed in Chapter 2.

5. Philipson, *The Reform Movement*, p. 81.

6. Hermann Schwab, *The History of Orthodox Jewry in Germany*, tr. Irene R. Birnbaum (London, Mitre Press, 1950), pp. 31, 48.

7. *Judaism Eternal: Selected Essays from the Writings of Rabbi Samson Raphael Hirsch*, ed. Isidor Grunfeld (London, Soncino Press, 1959), I, xxii–xxxviii.

8. *Ibid.*, I, xxi.

9. *Ibid.*, I, 210.

10. *Ibid.*, I, xlii.

11. *Ibid.*, I, xxxix–xliv; Schwab, *Orthodox Jewry*, pp. 63–66.

12. *Judaism Eternal*, I, xliv–xlv; Schwab, *Orthodox Jewry*, pp. 66–70.

13. Schwab, *Orthodox Jewry*, pp. 70–72.

14. *Ibid.*, pp. 75 f.

15. *Ibid.*, p. 73.

16. *Ibid.*, p. 78.

17. *Aboth* 2:2. For Hirsch's use of it, see *Judaism Eternal*, I, xv.

18. Samson Raphael Hirsch, *The Nineteen Letters of Ben Uziel*, tr. Bernard Drachman (New York, Bloch, 1942), pp. 4 f.

19. *Ibid.*, First Letter, pp. 5, 6, 7.

20. *Ibid.*, Second Letter, pp. 13, 14, 15.

21. *Ibid.*, Third Letter, pp. 20–22.

22. *Ibid.*, Third Letter, p. 29.

23. *Ibid.*, Fourth Letter, pp. 33, 34, 36.

24. *Ibid.*, Seventh Letter, pp. 66–70.

25. *Ibid.*, Eighth Letter, pp. 76 f.; Tenth Letter, p. 102.

26. *Ibid.*, Fifteenth Letter, pp. 146, 147, 148, 149.

27. S. R. Hirsch, "How Can We Carry Jewish Learning into Practical Life?" in *Judaism Eternal*, II, 282, 284.

28. *Nineteen Letters*, Fifteenth Letter, p. 157; Sixteenth Letter, pp. 159, 161, 164–65.

29. *Ibid.*, Seventeenth Letter, p. 174.

30. S. R. Hirsch, "Religion Allied to Progress," *Judaism Eternal*, II, 236 f.

31. *Ibid.*, p. 237.

32. Schwab, *Orthodox Jewry*, pp. 48–59.

33. See Alexander Marx, "David Hoffmann," in *Essays in Jewish Biography* (Philadelphia, Jewish Publication Society, 1947), pp. 185–222.

34. Schwab, *Orthodox Jewry*, p. 132, n. 15.

35. See numerous references to Leeser in Moshe Davis, *The Emergence of Conservative Judaism: The Historical School in 19th Century America* (Philadelphia, Jewish Publication Society, 1963), including a brief biographical sketch, pp. 347 ff. See also Maxwell Whiteman, "Isaac Leeser and the Jews of Philadelphia," *Publications of the American Jewish Historical Society*, XLVIII (1959), 207–44.

36. Leeser's first sermon is quoted in Joseph L. Blau and Salo W. Baron, *The Jews of the United States, 1790–1840: A Documentary History* (New York, Columbia University Press, 1963), II, 578–82. The two-volume collection of Leeser's sermons is entitled, *Discourses, Argumentative and Devotional, on the Subject of the Jewish Religion, Delivered at the Synagogue Mikveh Israel, in Philadelphia,* published in Philadelphia, 5597 (1837). See Blau and Baron, *The Jews of the United States,* II, 662, n. 176.

37. Leeser's description of these materials is quoted in Blau and Baron, *The Jews of the United States,* II, 449, from Leeser's *Instruction in the Mosaic Religion,* tr. from the German of Joseph Johlson (Philadelphia, 1830). See Blau and Baron, *The Jews of the United States,* II, 637, n. 105.

38. M. Davis, *The Emergence of Conservative Judaism,* pp. 59 ff.

39. *Occident,* I (1843–44), 457–62; 517–21; 567–73. Typical of the opposition to union is the following resolution, adopted by Congregation Beth Elohim of Charleston, S.C., August 10, 1841: "Resolved

that all conventions, founded or created for the establishment of any *ecclesiastical authority* whatever, . . . are alien to the spirit and genius of the age in which we live, and are wholly inconsistent with the spirit of American Liberty." Quoted from the minutes of Congregation Beth Elohim by Joseph Buchler, "The Struggle for Unity: Attempts at Union in American Jewish Life, 1654–1868," in *American Jewish Archives*, II (June, 1949), 27.

40. *Occident*, V (1849–50), 63. Italics in the original.

41. *Occident*, I (1843–44), 572.

42. Lilienthal's attack was published in Isaac M. Wise's paper, *The Israelite*, of which Lilienthal was corresponding editor. It is given here as reprinted by Leeser in the *Occident*, XIV (1856–57), 379–81. The quotation is from p. 381.

43. *Occident*, XIV (1856–57), 382.

44. *Jewish Messenger*, II (October 23, 1857), 68.

45. M. Davis, *The Emergence of Conservative Judaism*, pp. 233–41.

46. Gilbert Klaperman, "Yeshiva University: Seventy-five Years in Retrospect," *American Jewish Historical Quarterly*, LIV (1964–65), 5–52, is very good in its discussions of the "modern" or "secular" studies introduced into the Yeshiva.

47. Leo Jung, "What Is Orthodox Judaism?" in *The Jewish Library*, 2d series, ed. Leo Jung (New York, 1930), pp. 114 f.

48. Leo Jung, in *Judaism*, ed. Aaron Opher, a study course published in mimeographed form by the National Council of Jewish Women (1945), p. 5.

NOTES TO CHAPTER 4: THE COMPLEX PHENOMENON
OF CONSERVATIVE JUDAISM

1. W. Gunther Plaut, *The Rise of Reform Judaism* (New York, World Union for Progressive Judaism, Ltd., 1963), p. 19, taken from *Wissenschaftliche Zeitschrift für jüdische Theologie*, ed. A. Geiger (Frankfort, 1835), I, 1 ff.

2. Plaut, *Rise of Reform Judaism*, p. 21, taken from *Die Allgemeine Zeitung des Judenthums* (Leipzig), ed. Ludwig Philippson, I (July 27, 1837), 161 ff.

3. Plaut, *Rise of Reform Judaism*, p. 22, from *Archives Israélites de France*, ed. Samuel Cahen (Paris, 1840), I, 234.

4. Plaut, *Rise of Reform Judaism*, p. 23, from Z. Frankel, *Prospectus* (Berlin, 1843), pp. 5 f.

5. Louis Ginzberg, *Students, Scholars and Saints* (Philadelphia, Jewish Publication Society, 1928), p. 202.

6. Plaut, *Rise of Reform Judaism*, p. 24, from *Zeitschrift für die religiösen Interessen des Judenthums* (Berlin, 1844), I, 265.

7. For a discussion of Frankel's career, see L. Ginzberg, *Students, Scholars and Saints,* pp. 195–216.

8. David Philipson, *The Reform Movement in Judaism* (New York, Macmillan, 1907), pp. 221–25.

9. *Ibid.,* pp. 268–70.

10. Plaut, *Rise of Reform Judaism,* p. 86, from *Protokolle und Aktenstücke der zweiten Rabbiner-Versammlung, July 15–28, 1845* (Frankfort, 1845), pp. 18 ff.

11. See Moshe Davis, *The Emergence of Conservative Judaism: The Historical School in 19th Century America* (Philadelphia, Jewish Publication Society, 1963), Introduction, pp. 3–20.

12. Cyrus Adler and Aaron M. Margalit, *With Firmness in the Right: American Diplomatic Action Affecting Jews, 1840–1945* (New York, American Jewish Committee, 1946), pp. 3–8. Joseph L. Blau and Salo W. Baron, *The Jews of the United States, 1790–1840: A Documentary History* (New York, Columbia University Press, 1963), III, 924–55, contains relevant documents from Jewish and Christian sources. See also M. Franco, "Damascus Affair," *The Jewish Encyclopedia,* IV, 420 f.

13. Adler and Margalit, *With Firmness in the Right,* pp. 299–322.

14. See Cecil Roth, *A Short History of the Jewish People* (London, East and West Library, 1948), pp. 380 f.

15. See Gotthard Deutsch, "Mortara Case," *The Jewish Encyclopedia,* IX, 35 f.; and Bertram W. Korn, *The American Reaction to the Mortara Case: 1858–1859* (Cincinnati, American Jewish Archives, 1957).

16. Davis, *Emergence of Conservative Judaism,* p. 101, quoted from *Occident* (February, 1859), XVI, 541 f., and *American Israelite* (February 11, 1859), V, 244.

17. Davis, *Emergence of Conservative Judaism,* pp. 102 f.

18. *Ibid.,* p. 103, quoted from *Jewish Messenger,* VI (December 2, 1859), 164–66.

19. See Davis, *Emergence of Conservative Judaism,* pp. 101–8, 197–99, 200.

20. *Ibid.,* pp. 219 f., where Davis notes the difference in the attitudes expressed in articles published in the *American Hebrew* before the banquet and after it, viz., XV (July 27, 1883), 122, and XV (August 10, 1883), 146.

21. See Joseph L. Blau, *Cornerstones of Religious Freedom in America,* rev. ed. (New York, Harper & Row, 1964), pp. 205–12; and Leo Pfeffer, *Church, State, and Freedom* (Boston, Beacon Press, 1953), pp. 208–10.

22. Quoted by Davis, *Emergence of Conservative Judaism,* pp. 202 f., from *American Hebrew,* II (1880), 38.

23. Quoted by Davis, *Emergence of Conservative Judaism,* p. 202, from *American Hebrew,* I (1879), 38.

24. See the "Report of Committee on Choral Singing," quoted in Blau and Baron, *The Jews of the United States,* II, 494 ff. See also David and Tamar de Sola Pool, *An Old Faith in the New World* (New York, Columbia University Press, 1955), pp. 152 f.

25. Davis, *Emergence of Conservative Judaism,* pp. 210–12.

26. Alexander Kohut, *The Ethics of the Fathers* (New York, privately printed, 1920), pp. 16 f., 48, 7, 9. Italics in original.

27. For the Kohler-Kohut controversy, see Davis, *Emergence of Conservative Judaism,* pp. 222–28, and Albert H. Friedlander, *Reform Judaism in America: The Pittsburgh Platform* (New York, Union of American Hebrew Congregations, 1958), pp. 13 ff.

28. Davis, *Emergence of Conservative Judaism,* p. 239. Italics in original.

29. Irving Aaron Mandel, "Attitude of the American Jewish Community Toward East European Immigration," *American Jewish Archives,* III (1950), 31 f.

30. Charles I. Hoffman, "Memories of Solomon Schechter," in *The Jewish Theological Seminary of America,* ed. Cyrus Adler (New York, 1939), p. 64.

31. Solomon Schechter, *Seminary Addresses and Other Papers* (Cincinnati, Ark Publishing Co., 1915), p. xi.

32. *Ibid.,* p. viii.

33. United Synagogue of America, *Report of First Annual Meeting* (New York, United Synagogue of America, 1913), pp. 17, 19.

34. Cyrus Adler, *Lectures, Selected Papers, Addresses* (Philadelphia, privately published, 1933), p. 251, quoted by Marshall Sklare, *Conservative Judaism: An American Religious Movement* (Glencoe, Ill., Free Press, 1955), p. 290, n. 41.

35. United Synagogue of America, *Report of the Second Annual Meeting* (New York, United Synagogue of America, 1914), p. 26, quoted by Sklare, *Conservative Judaism,* p. 291, n. 57.

36. Solomon Schechter, *Studies in Judaism: First Series* (Philadelphia, Jewish Publication Society, 1938), pp. xix–xx, quoted in Bernard Mandelbaum, *The Wisdom of Solomon Schechter* (New York, Burning Bush Press, 1963), p. 102.

37. S. Schechter, *Studies in Judaism: Second Series* (Philadelphia, Jewish Publication Society, 1938), p. 116, quoted in Mandelbaum, *Wisdom of Solomon Schechter,* p. 103.

38. Sklare, *Conservative Judaism,* pp. 66–82.

39. See Morris Silverman, "Report of Survey on Ritual," in *Proceedings of the Rabbinical Assembly of America,* IV (1933), 322–43. A more recent survey, reported by Rabbi Morris S. Goodblatt in 1949,

indicates considerable progress in introducing a uniform prayer book after the publication of the Rabbinical Assembly-United Synagogue of America prayer books (*Sabbath and Festival Services* [Hartford, 1936]; *High Holiday Prayer Book* [Hartford, 1939]). In other respects, Rabbi Goodblatt's report shows that the earlier trends recorded here persisted. See Goodblatt, "Synagogue Ritual Survey," in *Proceedings of the Rabbinical Assembly of America,* XII (1949), 105–9.

40. Morris Silverman, "Report of Survey on Ritual," p. 130.
41. Indianapolis *Jewish Post,* May 21, 1948.
42. Milton Steinberg, *A Partisan Guide to the Jewish Problem* (Indianapolis, Bobbs-Merrill, 1945), p. 166.


NOTES TO CHAPTER 5: ZIONISM: FROM RELIGIOUS
NATIONALISM TO NATIONAL RELIGION

1. John Milton, *Paradise Regained,* Book Three, line 434.
2. Yehudah Halevi's *Book of Kuzari,* tr. Hartwig Hirschfeld (New York, Pardes Publishing House, 1946), Part II, Section 13, p. 78.
3. An interesting discussion of the theme of restoration is to be found in Franz Kobler, *The Vision Was There* (London, World Jewish Congress-Lincolns-Prager, 1956), p. 37.
4. Isaac Goldberg, *Major Noah: American-Jewish Pioneer* (New York, Knopf, 1937), p. 194. See also Joseph L. Blau and Salo W. Baron, *The Jews of the United States, 1790–1840: A Documentary History* (New York, Columbia University Press, 1963), III, 894–905, for Noah's "Proclamation" in 1825, and subsequent unfavorable reactions in the United States and Europe.
5. See Samuel H. Levine, "Palestine in the Literature of the United States to 1867," and Milton Plesur, "The American Press and Jewish Restoration During the Nineteenth Century," in *Early History of Zionism in America,* ed. Isidore S. Meyer (New York, American Jewish Historical Society and Theodor Herzl Foundation, 1958), pp. 21–38, 55–76.
6. See Howard M. Sachar, *The Course of Modern Jewish History* (Cleveland, World, 1958), pp. 60–65, for a summary of Napoleon's questions to the Sanhedrin; for the exact text of the questions, see W. Gunther Plaut, *The Rise of Reform Judaism* (New York, World Union for Progressive Judaism, Ltd., 1963), pp. 71 f., taken from the translation in the *Yearbook of the Central Conference of American Rabbis,* I (1890–91), 80 f.
7. Plaut, *Rise of Reform Judaism,* p. 134, from L. Philippson, "What Is Judaism?" in *Allgemeine Zeitung des Judenthums* (1837), I, 2 f.

8. Plaut, *Rise of Reform Judaism*, p. 137, from D. W. Marks, in *Jewish Chronicle* (1845), II, 27 f.

9. Abraham Geiger, *Das Judenthum und seine Geschichte* (Breslau, Schletter'schen Buchhandlung, 1865–71), I, 9.

10. Plaut, *Rise of Reform Judaism*, p. 138, from S. Holdheim, *Neue Sammlung jüdischer Predigten* (3 vols., Berlin, 1852–55), I, 156 ff.

11. Plaut, *Rise of Reform Judaism*, p. 143, from Moses Gutmann, in *Literaturblatt des Orients* (January 9, 1844), No. 2, pp. 22 f.

12. David Philipson, *The Reform Movement in Judaism* (New York, Macmillan, 1907), p. 168.

13. *Ibid.*, p. 255.

14. *Ibid.*, p. 492.

15. Samson Raphael Hirsch, *The Nineteen Letters of Ben Uziel*, tr. Bernard Drachman (New York, Bloch, 1942), Sixteenth Letter, p. 161.

16. *Ibid.*

17. For the early interest of Simon Dubnow in Jewish minority rights (as a form of Diaspora nationalism), see S. M. Dubnow, *Nationalism and History: Essays on Old and New Judaism*, ed. Koppel S. Pinson (Philadelphia, Jewish Publication Society, 1958; paperback edition, Cleveland, Meridian Books, 1961).

18. *The Zionist Idea: A Historical Analysis and Reader,* ed. Arthur Hertzberg (New York and Philadelphia, Meridian Books and Jewish Publication Society, 1960), p. 23.

19. *Ibid.*, p. 21.

20. *Ibid.*, p. 107; see also S. W. Baron, "Jewish Ethnicism," in *Modern Nationalism and Religion* (New York, Harper, 1947), pp. 213–49.

21. *The Zionist Idea*, pp. 109 f.

22. *Ibid.*, p. 111.

23. *Ibid.*, pp. 113 f.

24. *Ibid.*, p. 114. For additional material on Kalischer, see Israel Cohen, *The Zionist Movement* (New York, Zionist Organization of America, 1946), pp. 54 ff.

25. *The Zionist Idea*, p. 130.

26. *Ibid.*, pp. 136, 137.

27. I. Cohen, *The Zionist Movement*, p. 56.

28. *The Zionist Idea*, ed. Hertzberg, p. 138.

29. See S. W. Baron and J. M. Baron, "Palestinian Messengers in America, 1849–79: A Record of Four Journeys," in *Jewish Social Studies*, V (1943), 115–62, 225–92 (including appendix showing individual contributions).

30. Hyman B. Grinstein, *The Rise of the Jewish Community of New*

York (Philadelphia, Jewish Publication Society, 1945), pp. 450 f.

31. Abraham J. Karp, "The Zionism of Warder Cresson," in *Early History of Zionism in America*, ed. Meyer, p. 13.
32. *Occident*, XI (1853–54), 434.
33. *Occident*, XI (1853–54), 487.
34. *The Zionist Idea*, ed. Hertzberg, pp. 145, 147.
35. *Ibid.*, p. 151.
36. *Ibid.*, p. 152.
37. *Ibid.*, pp. 179–81; texts of *Auto-Emancipation*, pp. 181–98.
38. I. Cohen, *The Zionist Movement*, pp. 65 ff.
39. G. W. F. Hegel, *Philosophy of History*, tr. J. Sibree (New York, Willey Book Co., 1944), p. 47.
40. Heinrich von Treitschke, *Politics*, tr. Blanche Dugdale and Torben de Bille (London, Constable, 1916), I, 12.
41. See Salo W. Baron, "The Modern Age," in *Great Ages and Ideas of the Jewish People*, ed. Leo W. Schwarz (New York, Modern Library, 1956), p. 355.
42. Quoted *ibid.*
43. Maurice Barrès, *Scenès et Doctrines du Nationalisme* (Paris, Plon-Nourrit, 1925), I, 94.
44. For a brief account of the Dreyfus Affair, see H. Sachar, *The Course of Modern Jewish History*, pp. 231–35. Robert F. Byrnes, *Antisemitism in Modern France. Vol. I: The Prologue to the Dreyfus Affair* (New Brunswick, N.J., Rutgers University Press, 1950) is an excellent study of the background.
45. *The Zionist Idea*, ed. Hertzberg, p. 218.
46. *Ibid.*, pp. 217 f.
47. *Ibid.*, p. 220.
48. *Ibid.*, p. 221.
49. For a discussion of Herzl and the early congresses, see I. Cohen, *The Zionist Movement*, pp. 71–86.
50. *Ibid.*, p. 78.
51. *Ibid.*
52. *The Zionist Idea*, ed. Hertzberg, p. 242.
53. The Balfour Declaration is reproduced as an illustration in Cecil Roth, *A Short History of the Jewish People* (London, East and West Library, 1948), p. 346.
54. *The Zionist Idea*, ed. Hertzberg, pp. 600, 601.
55. Marshall Sklare, *Conservative Judaism: An American Religious Movement* (Glencoe, Ill., Free Press, 1955), pp. 219 ff.
56. *The Hebrew Union College Journal*, November, 1896.
57. Compare the opposing essays in *Reform Judaism: Essays by Hebrew Union College Alumni* (Cincinnati, Hebrew Union College Press,

1949): Leon Fram, "A Zionist Interpretation," pp. 174–95, and David H. Wice, "A Non-Zionist Interpretation," pp. 196–205.
58. Baron, "The Modern Age," in *Great Ages and Ideas of the Jewish People*, p. 424.
59. Atlantic City *Jewish Record*, April 2, 1948.

NOTES TO CHAPTER 6: WAS EMANCIPATION A MISTAKE?
MID-TWENTIETH-CENTURY APPRAISALS

1. Quoted in Hyman B. Grinstein, *The Rise of the Jewish Community of New York* (Philadelphia, Jewish Publication Society, 1945), p. 462.
2. See Yitzhak F. Baer, *Galut* (New York, Schocken, 1947).
3. Compare Lewisohn's attitudes in *Israel* (New York, Boni, 1925) with those in *The American Jew: Character and Destiny* (New York, Farrar, Straus, 1950).
4. Arthur Cohen, *The Natural and the Supernatural Jew: An Historical and Theological Introduction* (New York, Pantheon, 1962), pp. 182, 183.
5. *Ibid.*, p. 184.
6. *Ibid.*, p. 185.
7. Eliezer Berkovits, *Towards Historic Judaism* (Oxford, East and West Library, 1943), p. 37.
8. *Ibid.*, pp. 37, 38.
9. *Ibid.*, pp. 44, 45.
10. See *The Zionist Idea: A Historical Analysis and Reader,* ed. Arthur Hertzberg (New York and Philadelphia, Meridian Books and Jewish Publication Society, 1960), pp. 159–65.
11. *Ibid.*, p. 262.
12. *Ibid.*, p. 266.
13. *Ibid.*, p. 267.
14. *Ibid.*, p. 266.
15. For more selections from Ahad Ha-am's writings, see *The Zionist Idea,* pp. 249–77; *Selected Essays,* tr. Leon Simon (Philadelphia, Jewish Publication Society, 1912); *Ten Essays on Zionism and Judaism,* tr. Leon Simon (London, George Routledge, 1922); *Ahad Ha-am: Essays, Letters, Memoirs* (Oxford, East and West Library, 1946). For a biographical study, see L. Simon, *Ahad Ha-am* (Philadelphia, Jewish Publication Society, 1960), and its bibliography.
16. *Franz Rosenzweig: His Life and Thought,* ed. Nahum N. Glatzer (New York, Schocken, 1953), p. 219. But see the entire essay, "On Being a Jewish Person," pp. 214–27.
17. *Ibid.*, p. 223.

18. Martin Buber, *Die Chassidischen Bücher* (Hellerau, J. Hegner, 1928), p. 658.

19. Buber, *Mamre: Essays in Religion,* tr. Greta Hort (Melbourne, Australia, Melbourne University Press, 1946), p. 173.

20. *Ibid.,* p. 113.

21. *Ibid.,* p. 114.

22. A similar view of the personal spiritual quality of Judaism is to be found in the work of Abraham Joshua Heschel, especially in *Man Is Not Alone* (Philadelphia and New York, Jewish Publication Society and Farrar, Straus, and Young, 1951) and *God in Search of Man* (New York, Farrar, Straus and Cudahy, 1955).

23. See Mordecai M. Kaplan,"The Way I Have Come," in *Mordecai M. Kaplan: An Evaluation,* ed. Ira Eisenstein and Eugene Kohn (New York, Jewish Reconstructionist Foundation, 1952).

24. M. M. Kaplan, *The Purpose and Meaning of Jewish Existence: A People in the Image of God* (Philadelphia, Jewish Publication Society, 1964).

25. *Ibid.,* p. 299.

26. *Ibid.,* p. 294.

27. For accounts of the dispute between Rabbi Louis Jacobs and the Chief Rabbinate, see the following articles in the New York *Times* in 1964: March 29, 5:1; April 19, 4:1; April 24, 9:1; May 3, 13:1; May 4, 8:4; May 6, 15:1; May 10, 21:5.

28. M. M. Kaplan, "The Way I Have Come," p. 296.

29. M. M. Kaplan, *The Purpose and Meaning of Jewish Existence,* p. 325.

30. *Ibid.,* p. 326.

31. M. M. Kaplan, "The Way I Have Come," pp. 305–8.

32. M. M. Kaplan, *The Purpose and Meaning of Jewish Existence,* p. 311.

33. *Ibid.*

34. *Ibid.,* p. 310.

35. Samuel Dinin, "Mordecai M. Kaplan's Concept of Organic Jewish Community," in *Mordecai M. Kaplan: An Evaluation,* pp. 54 f.

36. M. M. Kaplan, *Judaism in Transition* (New York, Covici-Friede, 1936), p. 302.

37. *Ibid.,* p. 303.

38. M. M. Kaplan, *Judaism as a Civilization: Toward a Reconstruction of American Jewish Life* (New York, Reconstructionist Press, 1957), p. 345.

39. New York *Times,* November 10, 1963, 45:2.

40. Israel Goldstein, "The Menace of Secularism in the Synagogue," in *Proceedings of the Twenty-ninth Annual Convention of the Rab-*

binical Assembly of the Jewish Theological Seminary of America (1929), p. 94.

41. Abba Hillel Silver, "Synagogue Versus Synagogue Center: The Temple Should Be a House of Prayer and of Study Rather than a Place of Entertainment and Amusement," *American Hebrew*, CXXV (June 28, 1929), 204.

42. Indianapolis *Jewish Post*, June 24, 1949.

43. M. M. Kaplan, "Need Rabbi and Social Worker Clash?", in *Opinion*, March 28, 1932.

44. Harry L. Glucksman, "The Synagogue Center," in *Proceedings of the Rabbinical Assembly of America*, IV (1933), 273.

45. Sidney Hook, "Naturalism and Democracy," in *Naturalism and the Human Spirit*, ed. Y. H. Krikorian (New York, Columbia University Press, 1944), p. 40.

46. The text of the Columbus Platform may be found in the *Yearbook of the Central Conference of American Rabbis*, XLVII (1937), 97–100; for the discussion of the Platform, see pp. 94–96, 101–14.

47. With certain exceptions, such as the faction known as the Neturei Karta.

48. Joseph Badi, *Religion in Israel Today: The Relationship Between State and Religion* (New York, Bookman Associates, 1959), p. 29, quoted from "Legislation and Law in the Jewish State," *Yavneh* (Jerusalem-Tel Aviv, April-May, 1949), p. 9.

49. Badi, *Religion in Israel Today*, p. 30, quoted from *Yavneh* (April-May, 1949), p. 9.

50. For accounts of religious struggles in Israel, see the following articles in the New York *Times*. On the problems of a Liberal synagogue in Kfar Shmaryahu in finding a hall for High Holyday services, October 12, 1962, 2:4; October 19, 1962, 8:5. On the struggle of the Bnei Israel, Jews of Indian descent, to gain equal marriage rights with other Israeli Jews, February 25, 1962, 15:1; February 23, 1963, 2:3; July 30, 1963, 4:4; August 6, 1964, 2:6; August 18, 1964, 23:1; August 22, 1964, 18:1; September 1, 1964, 11:1. On the decision that Brother Daniel, a Jew who had converted to Roman Catholicism and had become a monk, was not entitled to Israeli citizenship under the Law of Return, December 7, 1962, 1:7. On the case of Mrs. Eitani, whose citizenship was questioned because she had not formally converted to Judaism, January 19, 1965, 30:5; January 27, 1965, 34:5; January 28, 1965, 7:4; January 29, 1965, 3:5; February 8, 1965, 24:4. On the dispute over non-kosher food for the ZIM Lines steamship *Shalom*, July 12, 1963, 1:3; August 19, 1963, 4:4; November 24, 1963, V, 16:2. On disputes with the Neturei Karta, October 27, 1963, 44:3; October 29, 1963, 6:4;

October 30, 1963, 2:3; October 31, 1963, 2:3. On the kidnapping of Yosef Schuhmacher by his uncle, an Orthodox rabbi who feared for the child's religious education, February 19, 1962, 7:3; April 4, 1962, 10:3; April 17, 1962, 7:7; June 13, 1962, 38:2; June 22, 1962, 2:1; July 2, 1962, 1:2; July 3, 1962, 1:6; 9:1; July 4, 1962, 1:3; July 5, 1962, 13:1; July 6, 1962, 10:1; July 7, 1962, 2:7; July 8, IV, 6:1 (review); July 9, 1962, 7:5; July 17, 1962, 10:3; September 2, 1962, 5:1; October 20, 1962, 2:6; October 24, 1962, 3:4; October 27, 1962, 51:2; October 29, 1962, 18:3; November 9, 1962, 22:2; November 29, 1962, 40:1.

51. Marshall Sklare, *Conservative Judaism: An American Religious Movement* (Glencoe, Ill., Free Press, 1955), p. 46, n.
52. Salo W. Baron, "The Modern Age," in *Great Ages and Ideas of the Jewish People*, ed. Leo W. Schwarz (New York, Modern Library, 1956), p. 375.
53. Sklare, *Conservative Judaism*, pp. 62 f.
54. See Ascher Penn, *Yiddishkeit ein Amerika* (New York, Judaism in America Library, 1958), English foreword, pp. vii-xxv.
55. This suggestion, originally made by Arnold Toynbee in his *A Study of History*, was retracted by him in a later volume of the same work. See also Maurice Samuel, *The Professor and the Fossil* (New York, Knopf, 1956), a reply to Toynbee's characterization.

# Index